MW01109734

Throughout this book, Ryan Krause identifies many spiritual victories in the most difficult of circumstances. He has also presented the Lord's teaching in such a way that it is possible to reach even those who have not yet found Christ.

Maj. General Nathan J. Lindsay, USAF Ret.

Reflections from the Battlefield is a provocative and inspiring account of God's presence in a most unlikely setting. Looking back on my own experiences in Viet Nam as a Navy A-6 fighter pilot, I wish I would have had this book to help me through those times.

Capt. J. David Harden, USN Ret.

Having served as the Training Officer for the Mobilization Training Command at Camp Pendleton during Operation Desert Storm, I have witnessed firsthand the courage and dedication of the men and women in our military. This book is a testament of the power of God's will even in the crucible of combat.

Lt. Col. Mel Cratsley, USMCR Ret.

About the Author

Ryan Krause has served 15 years as a Hospital Corpsman in the Navy, having been deployed in Operation Iraqi Freedom twice: first in 2003 and again in 2004-05. He previously served in Somalia from 1992-93.

In addition to his current active duty assignment at the Naval Hospital at Camp Pendleton, California, he is also pastor of Generations Church in Wildomar, California, a congregation with a vibrant growing membership.

Reflections from the Battlefield is the byproduct of Ryan's experiences in OIF 1 and 2, which initially materialized in the form of e-mails sent from Iraq to family and friends on a weekly basis.

Cover Photo: LCPL Matthew Celotto stands the post on top of a building inside Camp Blue Diamond, Ramadi. Ten days later he was seriously wounded by an incoming mortar round which nearly took his leg and his life. By God's grace, he has now fully recovered and has been accepted and is attending the U.S. Naval Academy in Annapolis.

REFLECTIONS FROM THE BATTLEFIELD

by

Ryan J. Krause

Blest Press
San Diego, California

REFLECTIONS FROM THE BATTLEFIELD

Dedication

To my brothers and sisters who have given everything on the battlefield for a people they did not know—for a purpose bigger than themselves.

Today, because of their sacrifice, millions of Iraqi men, women and children will now have a chance for a better life.

Tonight, because of their sacrifice, millions of American men, women and children will be able to sleep…in peace.

Acknowledgements

First and foremost, thank you *Jesus* for loving me so much that you came to this earth and gave Your life for mine. I will spend my entire lifetime attempting to comprehend the magnitude of a love that big.

To my wife *Kellee:* You have been my best friend and the love of my life. Even when the storm was raging you stood firm. When I stumbled you picked me up. When I floated too high you brought me lovingly back to earth. You are my hero.

To my son *Cameron:* What can I say? God has brought us a long way, I love you with all my heart and strength.

To *Phil Presley:* Thank you, brother, for seeing the invisible and for helping me to see that in order to *do* great things for God you must *attempt* great things for God.

To *Tom and Emily Barton:* Thank you for believing so much in this project and for giving a first-time author, who writes the way he speaks, a chance.

To *Heidi Bracco:* Thanks for the inspiration in coming up with such a powerful title for my book.

To the *Hahn family:* Thanks for your friendship and love. Thanks especially to Jimmy for inspiring me to reach higher when it would be easier to give up and crawl into a corner—and, for allowing me to use your mug shot on the back cover, scary as it is!

To *Charlotte Buster:* your emails touched me when I needed it most.

To the *Mason clan:* Your friendship has truly been a gift from above. I could not have done what I did without your holding down the fort back home. Phil, you will always be my brother and dear friend. Thank, you.

To *Donna Langdon:* Thanks for helping me to keep it real and remember that sometimes you just have to throw your head back and laugh like a small child.

To my amazing *Generations church family:* You will never know how much it means to be your pastor and to watch God move in your lives. Thank you for your love.

To the *Marines, Sailors and Soldiers* of the 1st Marine Expeditionary Force: Words cannot express the admiration and respect I have for you. You do a job that no one else could do. You are simply the best!

Last, but certainly not least, to *Bill Carson*: Without you, holding this book in our hands would not be possible. God used you powerfully to "connect the dots." Your selfless love, prayers, and Christ-like example have touched Kellee and me countless times. God's best to you and your family.

Respectfully,
Ryan J. Krause

Table of Contents

Introduction

In the Old Testament, both Saul and David were anointed kings of Israel by Samuel the prophet, and both were valiant men of war on the battlefield. However, the demanding and challenging environment of combat produced very different results in the lives of these two men.

King Saul: The Picture of Disobedience

We read in 1 Samuel that God chooses Saul to be the first king of Israel:

> *"There was a man of Benjamin whose name was Kish the son of Abiel, the son of Zeror, the son of Bechorath, the son of Aphiah, a Benjamite, a mighty man of power. And he had a choice and handsome son whose name was Saul. There was not a more handsome person than he among the children of Israel. From his shoulders upward he was taller than any of the people."*
>
> —1 Samuel 9:1-2

Saul is hand-selected by God to lead the Israeli people as their first king. However, he established a pattern of disobedience almost from the beginning of his reign. His method was to act first, then consider God's commands.

Following Jonathan's attack on the Philistine outpost at Geba, the Philistines assemble a great multitude against Israel consisting of 3,000 chariots, 6,000 charioteers, and a force of soldiers as numerous as the sand on the seashore.

When the Prophet Samuel does not arrive at the appointed time, the soldiers of Israel become afraid and hide themselves in caves among the rocks. Saul, after waiting for the appointed seven days and seeing that Samuel has not yet arrived, takes matters into his own hands, making a burnt offering to the Lord.

Immediately following the offering, Samuel arrives and asks Saul, "What have you done?"

It is obvious Saul has operated in the flesh and presumed upon God, so Samuel rebukes him by saying,

> *"You have done foolishly. You have not kept the commandment of the LORD your God, which He commanded you. For now the LORD would have established your kingdom over Israel forever. But now your kingdom shall not continue. The LORD has sought for Himself a man after His own heart, and the LORD has commanded him to be commander over His people, because you have not kept what the LORD commanded you."*
>
> —1 Samuel 13:13-14

Not long after this, Saul again leans on his own wisdom, believing that his choices are better than those of God. Consequently, the Lord again rebukes Saul through Samuel:

> *"'I will punish Amalek for what he did to Israel, how he ambushed him on the way when he came up from Egypt. Now go and attack Amalek, and utterly destroy all that they have, and do not spare them. But kill both man and woman, infant and nursing child, ox and sheep, camel and donkey.'"*
>
> —1 Samuel 15:2-3

Unfortunately, Saul makes the choice to spare Amalek's king, Agag, as well as the best of the livestock, justifying it to Samuel by saying:

> *"But I have obeyed the voice of the LORD, and gone on the mission on which the LORD sent me, and brought back Agag king of Amalek; I have utterly destroyed the Amalekites. But the people took of the plunder, sheep and oxen, the best of the things which should have been utterly destroyed, to sacrifice to the LORD your God in Gilgal."*
> —1 Samuel 15:20-21

This time, Saul is not only disobedient, but he compounds his sin by casting blame on others. This proves to be Saul's fatal mistake as again the Prophet Samuel sharply rebukes him by saying:

> *"Has the Lord as great delight in burnt offerings and sacrifices, as in obeying the voice of the LORD? Behold, to obey is better than sacrifice, and to heed than the fat of rams."*
> —1 Samuel 15:22

Sadly, the Bible records that Saul's leadership and kingdom are defined by rebellion, pride, and disobedience.

David: A Man after God's Own Heart

From his introduction in the scripture, David seems to be at a disadvantage when compared to Saul. He is not even considered by his father Jesse as one that Samuel (or God!) would be looking for. He is the youngest of Jesse's eight sons, merely a boy at the time.

How could this boy possibly be the next king of Israel? God's plan for David is not for him to assume the

throne immediately, but rather to take him through a process of refining and instruction that ultimately transforms
him into the king God intends for him to be.

David immediately finds favor in Saul's eyes and is
chosen to be one of his armor bearers. David's first real test
comes as Goliath stands in opposition to and defiance of the
armies of Israel. David's absolute confidence in God's ability to strike down this evil representative of the Philistines,
and his refusal to wear the King Saul's armor, stands in
sharp contrast to the reality of the situation.

Goliath is capable of taking on 20 or 30 Israeli soldiers at the same time; a man who by his mere appearance
causes men to shake in their armor. One would think the
more armor and weaponry the better! However, David refuses to place any confidence in the preparations of man
and to trust completely in the Name of the Lord God Almighty.

> *"You come to me with a sword, with a spear, and with
> a javelin. But I come to you in the name of the LORD of
> hosts, the God of the armies of Israel, whom you have
> defied. This day the LORD will deliver you into my
> hand, and I will strike you and take your head from
> you."*
>
> —1 Samuel 17:45-46a

OK, let's try to put this into perspective. David, a
young teenager, having no armor, no sword, no spear, and
only a sling plus five small stones, stands before this beast
of a man and essentially cuts him to pieces with words! If
we didn't already know the story, most of us would see an
inevitable train wreck coming for David and Israel. Of
course, we know the outcome, and we cheer for David
every time we recount the story.

The lesson is not just for David but also for all those
around him. He could have gone before Goliath packing the

big guns, but what purpose would this have served? Even the greatest weapons and armor could not have made a difference for David with this Philistine.

Total trust in God is the only weapon that could defeat this adversary. David learns early on that such confidence in the Lord is the only way to achieve victory on the battlefield.

Some time later we find that David falls out of favor with Saul because of the king's red-hot jealousy of him. Of course, David's favor with the people stems from his favor with God. But, David finds himself on the run from Saul, living like a common criminal in the wilderness.

Initially, one might say, "That's not how this is supposed to work out for David; he strives to do what is right before God." But God has further lessons for David to learn; and again, His chosen setting is on the battlefield and on the run.

After Saul attempts on numerous occasions to kill David, you would think that in self-defense David would be ready for any opportunity to remove his adversary. As a matter of fact, those who are with David on the run have just this in mind when on two separate occasions David has the opportunity to kill Saul.

> *"Then the men of David said to him, "This is the day of which the LORD said to you, 'Behold, I will deliver your enemy into your hand, that you may do to him as it seems good to you.'"*
>
> —1 Samuel 24:4

Saul continues to try to take David's life without any cause except jealousy, so David and his followers remain on the run for a long time. By this point, David has already been anointed by Samuel as king over Israel. No one would have faulted or accused David of wrongdoing if he were to take the advice of his men and strike Saul down.

But David again refuses the way of the flesh and instead chooses the way of the Spirit. To take the kingdom in an act of revenge or self-defense would not be the way of God. After beginning his reign in the Spirit, how could he consider ruling it in the flesh? Consider the words of Paul to the Galatians:

> *"O foolish Galatians! Who has bewitched you that you should not obey the truth, before whose eyes Jesus Christ was clearly portrayed among you as crucified? This only I want to learn from you: Did you receive the Spirit by the works of the law, or by the hearing of faith? Are you so foolish? Having begun in the Spirit, are you now being made perfect by the flesh?"*

—Galatians 3:1-3

The Galatians received the Gospel by faith and by the Spirit and tried to perfect their faith by the works of the law. Not so for David, for God has taught him to be patient, to rely on Divine timing and—most of all—to walk by faith, obeying the voice of the Lord. David's response is one of Godly wisdom and character:

> *"The LORD forbid that I should do this thing to my master, the LORD anointed, to stretch out my hand against him, seeing he is the anointed of the LORD."*

—1 Samuel 24:6

In fact, as a gesture of goodwill towards Saul, David cuts off a small corner of the king's garment to show he harbors no intention of harming him. Even so, David's heart is filled with remorse.

Do David's actions seem to defy any trace of common sense? To those to whom much is given, much is required. God expects more from the one who will lead His people

and establish Israel as the measure of greatness in the ancient world.

The kingdom and character of these two men stand in
sharp contrast to one another. One is a product of the flesh,
pride, and disobedience, and the other is a work of the
Spirit. One is destroyed and cut off from memory while the
other is established forever as the emblem of obedience in
the blood-line of the Messiah.

Saul is a man after his *own* heart—David is a man after *God's* heart! The lessons of David and Saul's lives on
the ancient battlefields of Israel stand today as principles
for us in our walk with God. It is my hope that from this
point forward the insights and lessons I have gleaned from
my time in harms way will both minister and touch your
heart, your family and your ministry in a way that prepares
you for the inevitable tests of life.

"Greater love has no one than this, than to lay down one's life for his friends."

—John 15:13

Part 1

Chapter 1

In the Beginning

Since this is my first book, I really had no idea how to start. I have always heard it said that there is no better place to start than at the beginning!

The Bible starts with *"In the beginning God created the heavens and the earth."* (Genesis 1:1) John starts his Gospel with *"In the beginning was the Word, and the Word was with God and the Word was God."* (John 1:1)

So, it seemed logical to me to tell my story by following the same pattern. After all, His Book has been on the best-seller list for quite some time!

In the beginning…This automatically brings a question to the surface that must be answered—in the beginning of what? This *beginning* is God's process of shaping me and teaching me about Himself, and He did it on the potter's wheel in the middle of a battlefield.

My goal is to get people to look at established ideas, scriptural truths, and life lessons through the lens God has placed in front of me. My hope is that this unique perspective will be something that many of you will be able to identify with to bring you into a closer walk with Christ.

I would never say that serving on the battlefield is fun, or something that I jumped at the opportunity to be a part of. Life is hard and dangerous. Time away from family and home is heart wrenching and painful. Some come home with wounds that will forever change their lives, and some don't come home at all.

At this point in my life, I would never choose to go into harms way or to go fight in a war; nevertheless, in God's divine will and plan, I have found myself there often. The scriptures talk of the greater weight of glory that comes through difficulties and the trials we face in life.

> *"Therefore we do not lose heart. Even though our outward man is perishing, yet the inward man is being renewed day by day. For our light affliction, which is but for a moment, is working for us a far more exceeding and eternal weight of glory, while we do not look at the things which are seen, but at the things which are not seen. For the things which are seen are temporary, but the things which are not seen are eternal."*
>
> —2 Corinthians 4:16-18

Enduring lengthy separations from my wife and family as well as from church friends is not easy and sometimes comes with feelings of complete isolation and loneliness. Although we know the scriptures teach us that trials and the fires of life are what develop and shape us more into the image of Christ, no one ever asks for them.

We know they will come to every Christian. It is not a question of if they will come, but when. It is what we do in the midst of those hardships that define who we are in Christ and who we will become.

If we run at the first sign of trouble, we stay where we are, spiritually. We never gain a greater revelation of who God is. While we don't welcome trials or even desire to go through them, we do grow and mature, experiencing a greater and more intimate relationship with our Savior who endured horrible trials, even to the point of death, the death on a cross.

There are few circumstances which present the same kind of trials that life on the battlefield does. In the Bible,

David writes most of his Psalms from the perspective of the battlefield. The fact is that the overwhelming majority of David's writings have him crying out to God for deliverance from his enemies, and it would appear that David had a lot of enemies.

Could it be that the greater the man or woman of God will be, the greater the trials which forge his or her life? Could it be that God's classroom of trials and tribulations are what produces the final product of holiness and godliness into a person He can actually use for His glory? For David to be a man after God's own heart, it seems he first had to be a man acquainted with sorrows, trials and grief. It seems that in order to develop the character and compassion necessary to be a king, he first had to experience God's refining process—most of which occurred on the battlefield.

The battlefield is always an extended and prolonged struggle which carries the gravest of consequences and the greatest of triumphs. This is not to minimize the many other trials and tribulations that people face every day; it is simply to underscore the fact that few environments present such a multitude of hardships and trials for extended periods of time.

One of the training programs that United States Navy Hospital Corpsmen go through which prepares them for combat service with the Marine Corps is the Fleet Marine Force Enlisted Warfare Specialist training program. This training identifies the following elements found in a combat environment:

- Violent, unnerving sights and sounds
- Casualties
- Confusion and lack of information
- Isolation
- Communications breakdown
- Individual discomfort and physical fatigue

- Fear, stress, and mental fatigue
- Continuous operations
- Homesickness[1]

These factors of war are those which are common, everyday occurrences for troops deployed abroad who are engaged in armed conflict.

There are many different types of trials that we can experience as followers of Jesus Christ which can be identified with battlefield experiences. The fact is, as Christians, we will have trials; this is unavoidable. Jesus said to His disciples, *"In this world you will have tribulations, but be of good cheer, I have overcome the world."* (John 16:33)

Jesus, speaking to the churches of Smyrna and Philadelphia, in what is modern day Turkey, commended them for their endurance and character through their onslaught of heavy trails.

> *"I know your afflictions and your poverty-yet you are rich! I know the slander of those who say they are Jews and are not, but are a synagogue of Satan. Do not be afraid of what you are about to suffer. I tell you, the devil will put some of you in prison to test you, and you will suffer persecution for ten days. Be faithful, even to the point of death, and I will give you the crown of life."*
> —Revelation 2:9-10, NIV

Interestingly, the Greek word for Smyrna is *Smurnaios* which is from the root word Smurna, meaning "Myrrh." Myrrh is a costly fragrance obtained by making an incision in the bark of a shrub found in Arabia. Also interesting to note, the substance does not give off its aromatic scent until it is crushed.

---

[1] Fleet Marine Force Enlisted Warfare Specialist training program, Section 106, *Marine Corps Combat Leadership Fundamentals.*

It seems that Jesus was saying to those enduring the trials, "Your perseverance, though you have been crushed by the world, is a sweet smelling fragrance to Me." He counted them worthy of the crown of life. Smyrna and Philadelphia are the only two of the seven churches mentioned in Revelation that did not receive a warning or rebuke from Jesus.

So many things that we as humans learn are learned through the experience of life. I am reminded of a country song by John Michael Montgomery which says, "Life's a dance we learn as we go." While life is so much more than a dance, the song makes an interesting point.

As children, so many of us never really learned what "don't touch" meant until we touched and realized just how hot the stove was! As kids, we don't fully understand what "don't" or "no" means until we experience the "board of education applied firmly to the seat of understanding."

As teens, we are *sure* we know all things; yet, we don't fully understand that being home on time has a direct impact on our use of the car, the television, or the phone until we are "grounded" and cut off from the rest of the civilized (or not so civilized) teenage world.

As adults, we learn quickly that no job means no eat.

As Christians we learn through experience that a life lived without Christ is a meaningless and empty existence.

In the classroom of the battlefield, I learned more than I ever did in school from textbooks, lectures or teachers. Of course, the learning experience is somewhat enhanced when you pay attention in class! I have no problem paying attention to the Master Teacher as He skillfully leads me through His divine lesson plan that includes my every sense. This process has been enhanced by my involvement in some of the most memorable events in recent history.

While unknown to me at the time, God began shaping me on the battlefield several years before I came to know Him. I was serving as a Combat Hospital Corpsman with the 3rd Battalion, 9th Marines during Operation Restore Hope in Somalia from December 1992, to March 1993.

I volunteered to deploy with the Battalion wanting to get some real life experience and to see the world. And see the world, at least a small part of it, I did! The imagery and experiences of my time in Mogadishu and other parts of Somalia have been forever burned into my memory and written into the pages of my mind. The world I saw was exceedingly different from anything I had experienced to that point in my short 20 years of life.

I will never forget the suffering, the horrible conditions of poverty caused by the civil war that gripped the country. Years and years of war, anarchy and lawlessness left its mark on this once beautiful city. Although many of the buildings were crumbling and horribly bullet and mortar scarred, the evidence of the once strong Italian influence was still present in the architecture and design of the buildings around the airport, the seaport, and throughout the city.

In the aftermath of the turmoil in the land, very few structures resembled their former splendor. In this sprawling city of over one million citizens, many of the people lived in slapped together tin and wooden shacks packed between the skeletons of structures that were still standing. The roofs where covered in cardboard, cloth, dirt, and trash in a futile attempt to keep out the weather.

The market consisted of little stands set up in open plazas and along the streets with different trinkets and food being sold, none of which looked too appealing or appetizing to me. Every other stand was selling what is known as Kat, a plant that is dried out then smoked, giving the user an hallucinating type of high. A large portion of the residents would smoke Kat around the same time of the day as a type of social and cultural ritual.

Operations were very dangerous during this time as the people, namely the members of the warring clans, would become very bold in their opposition to our being

there. They would take pot shots at us from behind buildings, down alleys, and from crowds and then disappear into
the masses. Many of the details of the military conflict we
were involved in were accurately described in Mark Bow-
den's book, *Black Hawk Down*.

Although all of these things left an indelible impression on me, the one thing which stands out most promi-
nently was the smell that filled the air most of the time. It
was the pungent, horrible smell of human decay and raw
sewage that ran down the streets. The smell was so horrific
that in certain places in the city you could barely breathe.

I recall one particular time when on a patrol we were
passing by an open square. I was in the back of a five-ton
truck in the turret, keeping watch while we drove. We
slowly passed by this square and a horrible smell soon
filled our nostrils and became so bad that we could not help
but gag. The smell forced us to loose control of our stom-
achs and experience tightening in our throats—and there
was nothing we could do to make it stop. I wondered what
in the world could stink so badly.

It was not long before I found out. The smell was
coming from a pile of what, at first, I thought was trash, but
then quickly realized it was a pile of corpses. The people
were piling more on at the time, and one edge was being lit
on fire to incinerate those who had died. As we continued
on, there were more people headed in the direction of the
square with bodies wrapped in blankets. To this day, I have
never forgotten that scene—or that smell.

Our primary reason for being in Somalia was to re-
spond to the famine that was raging which had claimed
some 300,000 people.[1] When you see the devastating ef-
fects with your own eyes, it does something to you—inside.

---

[1]"Somalia," Microsoft® Encarta® Online Encyclopedia 2004, © 1997-2004 Mi-
crosoft Corporation. All Rights Reserved. Viewed 27 November 2004.

Another incident which further reinforced the gravity of the situation in Somalia happened about a month after I arrived. We were conducting security operations for a United Nations food convoy just outside the city of Baidoa, which is some 180 miles northwest of Mogadishu. We traveled about 50 miles west of Baidoa to a small village in the middle of the desert.

When we arrived all the people came out to greet us, elated to see relief. Once we unloaded the trucks and filled the silo with the food we had brought, the Chief of the village came up to our Convoy Commander with tears in his eyes. We couldn't quite figure out what he was saying but it soon became clear.

He was so grateful for what we had done that he was trying to give his daughter to the Captain as a sign of gratitude. After some convincing by the Captain that he already had a wife and that he was humbled by the offer, we finally departed. Of course after that, the Captain was the subject of much of our teasing!

The gratitude of these people at having received the simplest thing like bags of food was greater than I have ever seen in anyone. It was truly a matter of life and death for them.

Death was such a part of normal life for these people that I could not help but hurt inside for them. It was unfathomable for me coming from the United States in all its blessings and wealth to see people who wondered from day to day where their next meal would come from or if they would even survive.

Their minds were filled with questions like, "I wonder if my child will live through the night," or "I wonder if my daughter will be killed by the warlords as they fight for control of my neighborhood."

In America we are asking questions like, "I wonder if I'll get my promotion," or "What college should I go to," or "I wonder what color sofa will look best in this room?"

After experiencing these things in Somalia, I had a healthy new appreciation for the many blessings we have and for all the things we take for granted every day—little things like running water, electricity, heat and air conditioning and sleeping at night in relative safety.

Little did I know that this experience would be the beginning of what God would teach me about spiritual life from the podium of the battlefield. Though I would not know Christ until nearly three years later, He had already taught me a lesson about life that would never leave me and even to this day impacts my life and ministry.

I have now been in the Navy for almost 15 years, and most of that time has been serving as a Hospital Corpsman with the United States Marine Corps. I knew that my life in the military would take a drastic and sudden change when the events of 9/11 occurred.

I think every single person in America remembers exactly where they were and what they were doing on that day. This is, as I understand, much the same as it was for those people 60 plus years ago who remember where they were and what they where doing when Pearl Harbor was hit.

I remember hearing on the news as I drove to work that Tuesday morning what was happening in New York. After arriving at work everyone just sat in front of the television unable to move.

We all watched in shock and disbelief—watching and knowing that we were now at war as a Nation against a then nameless enemy. We all knew that day as we sat there that life in the military would never be the same. The days of routine training and routine deployments would come to an end, and life would consist of operations that would be anything but routine. We knew that the United States would spend as long as it took to hunt down those responsible and make them pay for what they had done to our country and its citizens.

This is what we all thought in our human understanding and flesh. However, God spoke to my heart like a wave crashing on the beach. He stirred emotions and thoughts in me that I had never felt before. He breathed a message into me that week that could not be contained, that would not wait.

I told my senior pastor, Larry Walker, what God was stirring inside me, and I could barely get the words out without choking up. I was so filled with God's Spirit that I truly knew—first hand—what Jesus meant by *"I tell you that if these should keep silent, the stones would immediately cry out."* (Luke 19:40)

I felt at that moment that if I didn't express what was inside me, there could very well be a symphony of stones doing a number in song around me! My pastor, who was extremely sensitive to the Spirit of God, saw what was going on in me and yielded the pulpit that Sunday morning to me.

What followed was beyond my own understanding. God spoke a message through me that I still can't believe even when I listen to the tape. This is not to pat me on the back in any way, for to take credit for what God spoke to His church that day would be wrong.

A warning and a spiritual call to arms ushered forth from my lips to the people with such passion, such urgency that I don't know how I made it through the whole thing. My spirit and heart seemed to let out a battle cry!

I sensed that God had pulled His protective hand away from our Nation for just an instant—that for just a moment He had allowed the unthinkable to happen. He did not cause it, but He allowed it for the purpose of saying, "Ok, now that I have your attention…"

There was a spiritual wake-up call happening of the magnitude that none of us was prepared for. In a sense, it was a Nineveh-type proclamation from the throne room of heaven where God was essentially saying to America: "I have had enough—enough of My people turning their back on Me when I am the reason this country is so blessed; enough of abortion, homosexuality, racism, hatred, greed, murder and every other kind of evil; enough distorting the truth of My Word to fit *your* lifestyle. Wake up America and realize that I am the Lord your God, and I will not strive with man's sinfulness forever!"

At the conclusion of this message, I physically felt exhausted. The people sat there looking shocked and stunned. One by one, each got out of his or her seat and came to the front in repentance and humility—including me. The Living God had read us the "riot act," and it was time to change. It was time to take our Nation back for Him.

I later found out that this same type of thing had happened all over the Nation in churches everywhere. There was a Nation-wide spiritual awakening happening before our very eyes. Unless this Nation repented from top to bottom, I sensed it would not be long before we experienced something even more horrible than the events of 9/11.

In both my spiritual life and military life, things would never be the same. The line had been drawn in the sand, and it was now up to us, God's people who are called by His Name, to carry out the mandate.

He was calling us to take prayer back to school; to overturn the sinful laws of abortion; to block legislation attempting to redefine marriage; to teach our children to fear God; and to honor our marriages and our families. He was calling us to extend His love to everyone regardless of what anyone looked like, smelled like or talked like; and to preach the truth of God's Word without apology, without compromise from our pulpits, our airwaves and our workplaces; and to no longer tolerate tolerance—the most dangerous word in the English language.

God never told us to tolerate sin and injustice. In fact, to tolerate sin is to condone sin, and to condone sin is to partner with sin. God had given many of us a new commitment to the truth—to live the scripture *"I am not ashamed of the Gospel"* each day of our lives.

I knew that I was headed for a military roller coaster ride in the months and years to come. I knew that it was only a matter of time before I found myself in Afghanistan or even Iraq. Even before 9/11 happened, we in the military knew it was only a matter of time before we went back into Iraq. Saddam had defied the United States and the world too many times, and patience was running out.

Now I find that I am well acquainted with the ancient land of Babylon as I have spent many days and nights there considering God's mysteries and truths as exemplified in and on the battlefield.

The classroom of the battlefield is nothing new for God's chosen leaders. As I study the scripture I find that many of God's chosen people and leaders where shaped and instructed in this manner.

I think of the examples of Abraham as he wandered through the ancient land of future Iraq, struggling and warring with the people, to get to the place that God would show him. I think of Moses and the Children of Israel as they sat through a 40-year lesson of God's shaping and teaching them to be one people and one Nation under Him.

And, of course, there is David, who learned all too well the lessons of life on the battlefields of Israel. God was shaping him and teaching him to become a man after His own heart.

The lessons God's people learned on the ancient battlefields of Israel stand today as principles for us in our walk with God as we face our own physical—and spiritual battles.

Chapter 2

50 Days in the Desert

"The voice of one crying in the wilderness: 'Prepare the way of the Lord; Make His paths straight.'"

—Luke 3:4

It was difficult for me to write this chapter as there were so many things that happened during my trip to the Cradle of Civilization. The mere fact that I found myself there was in itself a shock.

When God first called me to start a church in the late 90's, I ran from it and tried to ignore God's calling. I didn't do this because I was trying to be disobedient but rather because I was afraid of the overwhelming idea of pastoring a church.

I had seen all too well how many times my pastors had been beaten up in the ministry, not only by those outside the church, but especially by those within. I had witnessed first hand the toll that the ministry takes on families and marriages, and, needless to say, I was in no hurry to jump into that fire myself.

But, of course, the tugging of my heart by the Holy Spirit continued. I also justified my delay in acting on God's call by concluding that I could not start a church while still being in the military with all the hours and deployments that go along with it. Besides that, my primary spiritual gift is an evangelist, not a pastor.

Finally, in November 2001, God strongly put this call on my heart again and spoke to me and my excuses saying, "Are you going to lean on your own understanding, or are you going to trust Me?" That's all it took; I knew that I must obey the voice of God, trusting that He had all the details well in hand.

After much prayer and preparation, we had our first service on New Year's Eve, 2001, and officially began the work that is Generations Church. We met in our home for three-and-a-half months until the Lord opened an opportunity for a building 15 April 2002. Things were going wonderfully well until December when I was told that I would be deploying to Kuwait with my unit for a possible war with Iraq.

Now stop the press! I'm not supposed to deploy Lord; You said You had everything under control! You told me to plant this church. How can this be? Naturally in my own mind I assumed that when God called me to start a church it meant I would actually be there to minister. Deploying was not in my mind at all.

Most of the month of January 2003 I spent working 15 and 18 hour days preparing my battalion's medical section to deploy with 1200 Marines, and on 2 February 2003, I found myself on an airplane to the Middle East. I was beside myself wondering what in the world God was doing. Had He made a mistake? Had I made a mistake and not really heard His voice?

It's amazing how much we question when we are faced with a crisis that goes against our understanding of a situation. On 3 February I found myself getting off the plane at Kuwait International Airport and being hurried onto a bus with covered windows along with 50 others. I was tired, jetlagged, confused and not sure of much at the time.

Upon my arrival in Camp Coyote, two hours north of Kuwait city, I found myself in the ugliest, most barren and desolate place I had ever been. (That's saying a lot for a person from Wyoming!) We were living in circus looking tents that the locals had put up for us and eating Meals Ready to Eat or MRE's. I must have slept for 24 hours that first day, trying to shake the cobwebs out of my head.

The next challenge for me was to find God's purpose for my being there. As God would have it, a friend from my church was with me and worked for me in the Battalion Aid Station—my good friend Leslie Walker, a Third Class Petty Officer whom I had assigned to Bravo Company as a Corpsman.

That first week nothing much happened other than settling into our new circumstances and getting to work preparing for our push into Iraq, which we all knew was coming soon.

By the next Sunday evening, Leslie and I had started getting together at 8 p.m. in one of the empty tents to pray. There was absolutely nothing in this tent except three wooden boxes and wooden decking. It was cold and dusty. Since there is an eleven hour time difference between Kuwait and California, 8 p.m. Kuwait time would be 9 a.m. California time when Generations and other churches would be starting their morning services.

We began by praying for our church and for everyone in it that God would bless them and be among them during the service. We then prayed for ourselves and the coming conflict with Iraq. Finally, we prayed that God would bring more people to pray with us and to study His Word. That was Sunday night the 9th of February. Leslie and I had decided to get together each Sunday and Wednesday night at 8 p.m.

When Wednesday night came around we had one more person join us. We again prayed together and shared from God's Word and concluded by praying that God would send more people to join us for prayer and that He would send revival to our camp.

The next Sunday night we added two more to our group. I was excited; our little church had grown 150% in one week. Now that's church growth! We continued our pattern of praying for the churches back home, our families, our current situation and concluded by again asking God to send more people to join us.

By the next Wednesday evening we started meeting in the chow tent which had chairs and tables. This night we had 11 people join us for prayer and study. I shared a message from God's Word about the faithfulness of Abraham and that night God won a great victory as one of those with us accepted Jesus as Lord and Savior, praying the sinner's prayer at the conclusion of my message.

I was doing a little dance in my spirit—so excited about what God was doing. Those who were present began to experience a fire in their spirits for the Word of God and for fellowship that was contagious.

One of the young guys asked me at the end of the evening if we could meet *every* night for prayer and study. I couldn't believe my ears. Here was a young man only two months old in the Lord and already he had a passion inside him that made him glow with the radiance of Christ. I just looked at him not believing what I was hearing and said, "Absolutely!"

From that night on we met every night at 8 p.m. for prayer, study and fellowship. We began to experience the unmistakable presence of God and unity within our group. By the next Sunday night we had gone high-tech and added worship to our service. We had a portable CD player and two battery-powered, plug-in speakers.

I selected a number of songs and the place erupted with praise, all on their feet, all worshipping, oblivious to anything around them but the presence of God. I was so moved and humbled that I did not have words. This night we had 25 in the service and two accepted Christ.

Expectancy began to build in the camp for our services and an average of 20 joined us nightly for prayer. By the next Sunday evening 52 people came to hear God's Word and worship with five making decisions for Christ.

Now, I have experienced a lot of great church services and outreaches in my life, but nothing could compare at that moment to what God was doing in this place. There was a spirit of revival that I had not ever experienced or seen. The miracles that God was performing before my very eyes amazed and humbled me.

There were no comfortable chairs or nice carpeting. There was not a praise and worship team with the best speakers and instruments. There was not a temperature controlled clean building for us to meet in. It was raw, unrefined God Power—pure and simple—with Holy Spirit waves pouring over the people that could not be duplicated even if we tried.

This was a sovereign move of God's Spirit pouring out on us in this place more powerfully than in any stadium, church or Bible study I had ever attended. Being in the land of the Bible, I felt that I saw the unity, the joy, the fellowship that the early church must have felt. God's Word from Acts kept ringing in my mind:

> *"So continuing daily with one accord in the temple, and breaking bread from house to house, they ate their food with gladness and simplicity of heart, praising God and having favor with all the people. And the Lord added to the church daily those who were being saved."*
>
> —Acts 2:46-47

In most churches and Christian circles that I have been associated with there is the desire for revival and for an "Acts" type of experience. There is a strong desire to see a more simplistic and raw demonstration of God's power that rends people's hearts in two and compels them to call upon the Lord Jesus Christ for salvation.

Here I was, 12,000 miles away from home in an environment that seemed anything but conducive for an outpouring of God's Spirit, and there it was—just like I had always prayed and hoped for. The messages I preached were not fancy or complex, but yet the power of God through His simple Gospel message was bringing people to their knees.

> *"And I, brethren, when I came to you, did not come with excellence of speech or of wisdom declaring to you the testimony of God. For I determined not to know anything among you except Jesus Christ and Him crucified. I was with you in weakness, in fear, and in much trembling. And my speech and my preaching were not with persuasive words of human wisdom, but in demonstration of the Spirit and of power, that your faith should not be in the wisdom of men but in the power of God."*
>
> —1 Corinthians 2:1-5

There are so many examples of God's complete control of our situation that I could fill several books. A few weeks into this revival, one young man, Jonathan, who had been saved for only two months, came to me during the day and said he went around to all the tents putting signs up advertising and inviting people to our services. I was pretty excited to see his enthusiasm and zeal for God and told him as much.

That night we had over 50 people in attendance and the Spirit of God was moving on the people with power. At the conclusion of the service we had seven decisions for Christ.

God compelled me to open the floor to testimonies from the people. A sergeant who had just accepted Christ stood and began to speak. He told us of how his heart was hard and how he had been living a very hard and fast life. He was by his own words "an enemy of God" and for most of his life felt angry toward God, if there was one. He had some pretty rough things happen over the last week and the night before the service he had called out to God saying, "If You are real and if You are really there, show me a sign."

You probably can see where this is headed. That afternoon he was in the line at the chow hall and when he got to the entrance, there on the side of the tent was a "sign" that said, "Bible study and prayer, 8 p.m., chow tent." He continued, "That's all it took for me, and I knew I had to be here tonight no matter what. God has overtaken my heart and freed me from my anger—and my hard heart." There were several people tearing up, including me. I embraced him and thanked God for His amazing work in Sergeant Lopez's life.

Another person gave a testimony that night of how he was preparing to go and "hook up" with a female Marine who also was in the camp. He said that as he was on his way to meet her, he passed by our tent and heard the praise and worship with everyone singing.

He said he tried to pass by but something would not let go of him. He stood outside for a moment and felt as though he was caught in a tractor beam, powerless to go any further. He almost robotically moved into the tent and sat down. He said it felt as though he was being held down in his seat. "Somebody wanted to get my attention real bad tonight," he said. He was among the seven who accepted Christ that night.

Another stood and said he had been running from God for years. He grew up in a good Christian home, but once he joined the Marine Corps he fell away. He had been invited several times to our services but had refused. Tonight no one had asked him to come; he just knew he had to be there. That night he prayed a prayer of re-commitment to live for Christ.

The next morning I was talking to the Battalion Commanding Officer who is also a believer. I was telling him about the things happening in the Bible studies and how people where getting right with God. He asked what time the services were and I told him 8 p.m. He asked me if we were singing last night around that time. I said "Yes, last night was a wonderful worship service with everyone singing along."

He said that he had heard us from his tent and stepped out to listen for several minutes. The sound of God's people lifting up praises to God brought him comfort and peace.

Nearly every night in our prayer and fellowship group one or two would accept Christ. I was no longer the only one who was sharing from the scriptures; a number of others also were compelled to share what God was showing them in His Word.

One night in particular a young Marine by the name of Corporal Ryan asked if he could share something that was on his heart. Corporal Ryan had been drawn deeply into a personal relationship with God during these past few weeks of revival.

The interesting thing about Corporal Ryan is that he is a staunch Roman Catholic, loving his church and traditions deeply. I had seen a spark ignite in this young man that was amazing. He stood and, according to the common practice of his church, he shared an Old Testament reading and a New Testament reading.

He then began to "preach" the Word of God so powerfully and so passionately that the conviction of the Holy Spirit came over me as I listened. He talked about the duty that we as Christians have to display Christ to the world. He talked about how nothing else in life matters except pleasing God and pointing others to faith in Christ. He also pointed out that many of us were getting too focused on the number of people who were now attending the services and that we needed to focus on Christ instead.

I was certainly guilty of this more than anyone, and the Holy Spirit was speaking directly to my heart. At that moment I asked God to forgive me for getting off track and to re-focus me on Him. As a pastor, many times I can get so wrapped up looking at numbers and giving that I lose focus on the most important thing. My nature to "count the troops" was evident even in the midst of this revival.

Corporal Ryan continued his exhortation and concluded with a challenge for all of us to keep "first things first." You see, I wasn't the only one excited about the number of people coming. Our core prayer group of about 15 talked often about the numbers. We all were in a sense, "numbering the troops."

The message was God-breathed and powerful. All of us were convicted, and we spent the next two and a half hours praying that God would keep us focused on Him and let Him worry about the numbers. We prayed in our group in a freezing tent until after 11 p.m. and even then we were hesitant to stop.

This Roman Catholic brother had received the Spirit of the Living God and his whole nature, his whole countenance was changed. God revealed Himself to Corporal Ryan in a way that removed his "religion" and replaced it with Jesus.

I also distinctly remember another young man, a Lance Corporal who had been in the Marine Corps a little over a year. He was a tall, slender, awkward kind of guy with a child-like way about him. At 19 years old and very immature, he resembled a large puppy, still not sure of himself.

He had dirty blond hair and a little spotty mustache. He had come once or twice but had not really shown a lot

47

of interest and was kind of cynical during our studies. He always had a scowl on his face and smart remark.

One night as I shared from God's Word, I noticed something changing in him. As I spoke of the difference between the two thieves on the crosses next to Jesus and the danger of hardening your heart to God, he began to weep. I concluded in the next few minutes and looked at him face to face. I knew the rest of the guys were praying at that moment as I felt the power of the Holy Spirit upon me. I asked him if he was ready to say yes to Jesus. I said, "After all, He has already said yes to you."

He prayed at that moment and received Jesus into his heart. That in itself was amazing, but the most incredible part for me was seeing the smile that was on his face through his tears. It was the biggest, most beautiful smile I had ever seen. It was the smile of freedom and joy at what God had done. He was a tobacco chewer, so his teeth were yellow and dingy, but that smile could not have been more radiant and beautiful.

I will never forget what came next. I stood to embrace him and welcome him to the kingdom. He held on to me still sobbing and would not let go for a least a minute or two. I just hugged him and told him that God loved him so much and that he was now forever part of God's family.

Just recalling this incident and writing about it has flooded me all over again with the feeling I had at that moment. Nothing compares to a new life in Christ.

On one of the Sunday nights when we were having our service, there was a horrible dust storm going on outside that began right before the service started. The wind was beating the tent around and filled the inside with dust making it hard to sing and talk. We were 45 minutes into the service when there was a bit of a commotion in the back.

A Marine had undone the ropes on the door flap and came in late. I was a bit annoyed at the disruption because he was making a lot of noise as he came in. After the service I asked the Marine why he had been late—the nerve of someone interrupting me when I was preaching God's Word!

What he told me convicted me so deeply that I had to repent of my thoughts. He said that he had started out for the service from the other side of the camp earlier that night. The dust storm was so bad that he couldn't see two feet in front of him, and he soon became lost. He told me that he considered turning back and not coming but decided that nothing was going to stop him from being there. He stumbled around the camp for 40 minutes trying to get to the service.

You could have knocked me over with a feather. Back home people decide not to come to church if they are a little tired in the morning or if they have something better to do. Not even a blowing dust storm could stop this young man from getting together with God's people. Needless to say, I was never bothered by distractions again.

Another amazing example of what God did during this time was with a young sergeant who was a squad leader for Charlie Company. He had eight Marines in his squad besides himself. He was praying before the deployment that there would be Christians he could fellowship with when he got to Kuwait.

He was a sold-out Christian who was considering going into the ministry after the Marine Corps. This guy was so joyful and wonderful to be around as he exuded the love of Christ at all times. He was short and stocky—a man's man who was very motivated about the Marine Corps and leading his guys. He told me one night at the beginning of the revival that he was praying that all eight of his Marines would come to know Christ before the war started.

He couldn't stand the thought of going into combat knowing that any of them were not right with God. One by one he brought the members of his squad to the services, and each time he brought a new one, that one got saved—five in all accepted Christ up to the last week before the war started, a victory by any standard. But that was not good enough for the sergeant.

The last Sunday evening service prior to the start of the war was on the 16th of March. Many from the camp were already pushing forward to the border preparing for the offensive into Iraq. There were three last holdouts in his squad who had no intention of coming to church and were very hostile to religion of any type.

I don't know what he said to them or how he got them to the service, but three days before the ground war began, these last three Marines crumbled before the Lord and prayed to receive Christ. I was extremely excited, but that was nothing compared to the excitement this sergeant was experiencing as he saw God answer his prayer completely. All eight members of his squad were now born again!

When I think of his faith and how he believed God for all eight of his guys, I am filled with joy and amazement. His faith grew so much during those weeks leading up to the war seeing God answer his prayers, one Marine at a time. I often wonder if he did go into the ministry. I know his experience with God left a permanent mark on his life.

One by one, all six of our companies moved forward to the border in preparation for the ground war. The camp became mostly empty except for parts of Headquarters and Service Company of which I was a part. On the 19th of March as I was praying, God gave me a vision of our Battalion and this "force field" of His protection over them.

He spoke to my heart saying that, "Not one life will be lost in the battalion." I was overwhelmed with faith and knowledge that God had spoken to me, and I believed whole-heartedly that this would be a reality.

The ground war started that night with a strategic hit in downtown Baghdad in an attempt to take out Saddam himself. Our forces flowed over the border from Kuwait into Iraq from two points along the border. Several of our companies were attached to the 1st Marine Division directly on the front line of the attack.

From the time the war started to the time that Baghdad fell, not one of our Marines or Sailors was killed or wounded other than minor injuries! This is amazing when you consider that we were directly in contact with the enemy during some of the heaviest fighting to include An Nasiriyah.

All of our units and companies pushed forward in the days after the war started and 12 hours before I was to push forward with H & S Company, I received a Red Cross message from home. The message given to me by the battalion Chaplain around 2 p.m. on 22 March was from my wife; my heart sank.

Kellee's father John had suddenly died of a heart attack. I was so sad inside but even more so for my wife. I knew that she was a nervous wreck at home with the war just starting and then her father dying the next day. All I could think about was her and needing to be with her. Now that the war had started, I knew that the military would never let me go home, unless an immediate family member had died.

As I processed what had happened the chaplain gave me the satellite phone to make a call home. I had only talked to Kellee once since being gone; so, this would be very unusual. As I spoke to her on the phone I could tell she was horribly stressed and hurting. I longed more than anything at that moment to be with her and hold her, telling her that everything would be OK. When I got off the phone, the chaplain asked what I wanted to do. I said, "What do you mean?" He said that he had talked to the Executive Officer who was still there and that if I wanted to go home I could.

It was then that I had a moment of crisis. I am the Chief for the battalion and responsible for all my guys.

They had all just pushed forward into a war, and we didn't know how long it would last or what the outcome would be. He said, "Pray about it and tell me in an hour."

I went to my cot and began to seek the Lord for what He would have me do. I wanted more than anything to be with my wife, but I felt a strong sense of guilt about leaving my guys during the war.

Another Chief, Wayne Brown, had deployed with me and was going to be my relief when I had to transfer back to the states in May. He had been there all along and was a more experienced Chief than I. That was it then. God had already placed the solution right before me. Wayne was already in place, well acquainted with the guys and probably more able to do the job than I was.

I went back and told the chaplain that my decision was to go home. He said, "I knew you'd make the right choice." I said, "What do you mean?" He said, "Your replacement has been here all along." God had confirmed my choice and within two hours I had turned over all my gear and passed on all necessary instructions to my Leading Petty Officer and was on my way to Kuwait City and home to my wife.

My anticipation for the reunion with my wife was something that God would speak to me about later. His desire to be with us is even greater than my desire to be with Kellee. He longs for that intimate fellowship and communion with His bride and looks with anticipation to each time we take time to spend with Him. He loves us so much, and there is nothing He wants more than to be with us.

During that time, God showed me a small glimpse of the great anticipation He has to be with us, and every time we commit to spend that intimate time with Him in prayer and meditation it's like the wonderful joy and excitement I was experiencing with the thought of being reunited with my Kellee.

He loves to surprise us and bless us. He loves to shower us with the best things in life and sweep us off our feet. Yes, in the smallest way, God was telling me that the feeling of anticipation that was rising up in my soul with every passing hour is the way His heart yearns for us each moment. We have a God who loves us that much!

God's perfect timing brought me home after 50 days. I had been studying Genesis together with Kellee, one chapter a day while I was gone. It is no coincidence that the account of the Exodus and God miraculously bringing Moses and the Children of Israel out of Egypt reminded me of my own miraculous exodus from the Middle East. God's timing was perfect and amazing.

During the 50 days I spent in Kuwait, God taught me many things. Following my return, I traveled to a number of churches sharing what God had done and what He had revealed to me. The results were wonderful as many people's lives were changed because of God's message of hope and revival.

As nearly as I can recollect from my time in Kuwait, 35 people made confessions of faith in Jesus Christ. 13 prayed prayers of re-commitment to Christ to get back on track where they had been back sliding in their walk with Him. By our last service there were more than 100 people in attendance, many of whom where strengthened in their relationship with Jesus.

There were also 11 people who were baptized. You may recall seeing pictures in the media of the baptisms that were taking place all over Kuwait prior to the start of the war. We were among them. All of this is not to focus on numbers, but to focus on the awesome working of God during this 50 day period of time. The work He did will forever stand in my mind as a miracle.

Chapter 3

Operation Iraqi Freedom 2-2

I wondered for a long time what my second deployment to Iraq would be like—still vivid were the memories from my short time in Kuwait. The thoughts of the great move of God's Spirit upon the Seventh Engineer Support Battalion prior to the war to protect the entire battalion in a not so certain environment was still fresh on my mind.

Now working in the Emergency Department of the Naval Hospital Camp Pendleton, I had been given a seven month notification that I would be deploying again. In the time that led up to my departure I began to envision great things that God would do.

If God could pour out such revival in only 50 short days leading up to the war, imagine what He could do in seven months when I would be permanently stationed inside the borders of Iraq. Imagine the lives that could be changed and the great power He could display in the daily face of battle.

To be honest, I was a little nervous about going this time. The landscape of the war had changed considerably since I had been there the year before. Then we were engaged with conventional military forces and normal battlefield tactics. Now it was all different. Rather than face tanks and artillery, we were facing a stealthy force of radical insurgents bent on making our lives a living hell.

Their tactics were something that we had not encountered in any other conflict before. This was the type of thing that other countries were accustomed to—not us.

It reminded me of my time in Somalia over a decade earlier. We were engaged by nameless foes that fired at us from behind buildings and crowds of people. They wore no uniforms so generally you could not tell who was friendly and who was not.

We were engaged in urban warfare doing house-to-house raids. Our convoys were coming under attack almost daily by Improvised Explosive Devices (IED) and suicide bombers. I was sure God could do mighty things, but it was the environment that worried me.

When I first received word that I would be going, I had no idea what my job would be or where I would be located once I got to Iraq. I had been a line company corpsman in Somalia with an infantry battalion, so I knew what that could entail for our guys.

The year before, I had been the Battalion Leading Chief Petty Officer for the Seventh Engineer Support Battalion's aid station. I was in charge of preparing our Marines medically and assigning my own line company corpsman to their companies.

This was a very difficult task because I knew there were three companies that would be directly in the line of fire on the front lines of the war. As a leader, making these assignments carried with it the very real possibility of my guys being wounded or killed in action. As the Chief, I held the final decision, and that is no small matter.

I became aware of the wives and family members of all my guys back home who, on the day we left Camp Pendleton, looked at me with such hope and fear at the same time. All of them were saying the same thing; "Please make sure he comes home to me." Although this was not ultimately up to me, I inevitably found myself making them promises that were not mine to make. "I will bring them all home, I promise."

The weight of this promise was upon me over and over as I pushed them to be the best. I insisted that they continually train for mass casualty type events. I also insisted that they train their Marines how to be litter bearers for the wounded and to be "Combat Aidsmen."

This is a type of training given to Marines which prepares them to do basic first aid and buddy aid for their fellow Marines on the battlefield. It is necessary because per line-company of 100 or so Marines there were only two corpsmen assigned. In some cases there would not always be a "doc" available right away.

I pushed them hard because I knew the stakes were high. Not only did I want them to be prepared for anything that could happen on the battlefield, but also I wanted to honor my promise to their families back home.

The rules of the war were different this time. I saw Iraq as a great big Somalia—so many things unsure and unknown.

For months as I worked with my crew in the Emergency Room, I had to make hard choices about who would deploy again. It seemed like on a weekly basis I got another tasking from the Manpower Mobilization department telling me that they needed another one of my guys to go to Iraq.

This became a challenge for me, as I had to juggle the personal issues of each Sailor with the reality that I may have to send him into war. I also had to continue to run the department and keep the ambulances and the emergency room staffed. This became an exercise in futility with the war demanding more and more personnel to replace those who had been wounded in action.

Before long we had to cut back the number of "rigs" that were operating and put our staff on 24 on/24 off shifts. My staff was exhausted and more requirements were coming in all the time. How much more could we sustain and still operate the department?

Tough times often call for tough measures to be taken. We came up with creative new ideas for keeping the crew going and providing the level of care that was necessary in an emergency environment. Ultimately, my time came as well, and I found myself back with the First Force Service Support Group ready to deploy again.

My job this time would not be a battalion Chief. Instead I would be the Patient Evacuation Coordinator for the entire Al Anabar district of Iraq with which the 1st Marine Expeditionary Force was charged. This region stretched from just west of Baghdad all the way to the Syrian and Saudi Arabian border. I would be positioned inside the 1st Marine Division Headquarter in Ramadi, Iraq with the Commanding General's staff.

I had the enormous responsibility of moving all casualties occurring within this area of operation which included such hot beds as Fallujah, Ramadi—and the always contentious area around Abu Ghraib prison.

This was all situated in the now famous "Sunni Triangle" where the majority of insurgent activity was occurring. Fallujah had already become famous in world media for its heavy population of insurgents and the suspected headquarters of notorious Al-Qaeda operative, Jordanian-born Abu Musab al-Zarqawi, whose militant group was responsible for dozens of attacks on coalition forces and civilians.

I could not ignore the gravity of my situation. My team and I had a short turnover with the standing crew, and by the 1st of September we were in full swing with moving casualties off the battlefield.

I immediately found that God had placed me in a position of great responsibility both militarily and spiritually. My military duties were sobering and demanding with 90% pertaining to bad things that happened to our forces. The days were long and emotionally exhausting as hour after hour we dealt with the reality of the danger to our troops on the ground.

I found myself praying for each Marine, Soldier, and Sailor as their names came across my desk. As we prioritized them according to the severity of their injuries and dispatched helicopters to pick them up, the list of wounded began to take a toll on all of us. We would move with lightning fast reflexes to make decisions on the spot that would ultimately determine whether a service member lived or died.

We knew with the kind of injuries we were dealing with that getting them to the closest operating table and surgeon was their only chance of survival. Gun shot wounds, shrapnel, amputations, blast wounds, and burns were commonplace each day.

Each soldier was someone's son or daughter. Many were husbands or wives with kids at home. All were important to someone who loved them. Each had his or her own story, and it was now up to us to make sure that story did not end. At least that is how we approached each one who came in to us.

During these times you can't help but think about the information you have in front of you. It's as though time stands still for a moment and the implications of the situation begin to flood your mind. We were the first to get information about a service member who was wounded or killed. Within 24 to 36 hours someone back home would receive a visit from an official within the chain of command.

The thoughts of a representative in a dress uniform pulling up in front of a home, making his way to the front door with the worst possible news was on my mind constantly. I prayed for those wives and kids and loved ones who would answer the door and find their lives forever changed.

The burden I had as I moved the wounded was to pray fervently for God's healing touch to be on them and sustain them; it was sometimes more than I could bear.

On more than one occasion I found myself so mentally and emotionally drained that I could barely function. It was surely only by the grace of God that I was able to continue.

Often I thought of those on the ground who were friends and brothers in arms with those who had fallen. I thought of the medics and corpsman who struggled against time to save the lives of those in their charge, helpless amid the sight of horrific wounds and carnage as people were sometimes blown to pieces.

I remembered my own experiences when I was a line company corpsman of literally holding Marines in my arms, praying they would not die—seeing the look of fear in their eyes as they realized their condition—seeing the toll on those around them as they saw one of their own placed on a litter or in a body bag.

All of these things raced through my mind each time a call came in. Some days there were very few calls. Some days there were more calls than we could handle. Nearly everyday we would have a "fallen angel" on the battlefield. (This was the term we used for those killed in action.) I could feel the pain and the loss of those on the battlefield.

Although I was not treating casualties, my job directly affected every casualty. Whereas unit corpsman and medics dealt occasionally with those wounded or killed, I dealt with them each and every day.

My prayer life intensified dramatically. The prayers I offered up to the God of Heaven were sometimes no more than a sob, many times without words. It reminded me of the scripture which says:

"In the same way, the Spirit helps us in our weakness. We do not know what we ought to pray for, but the Spirit himself intercedes for us with groans that words cannot express."

—Romans 8:26

I was experiencing the reality of this scripture truly for the first time in my life. So many times I had no idea what to pray. My heart was crushed inside in a way that I could not express to God in words the depth of the sorrow and pain I was feeling for each of these wounded or killed and their families.

I would pray and pray, many times not being able to form words, yet still experiencing a torrent of prayer pouring through me to God. It was like a great river of rushing water bottled up behind a dam that is ready to burst. When you open your mouth the sound is unknown to you or anyone else, but it is known in the throne room of God.

The Holy Spirit is the Father's agent here on earth who lives inside us and takes the information from our hearts and minds and translates it clearly to God. It is as though He says, "Father, this one is full; he can't tell you what he is feeling but I can. This is the prayer of his heart."

Another example from the scripture comes to mind in this:

> *"Two men went up to the temple to pray, one a Pharisee and the other a tax collector. The Pharisee stood and prayed thus with himself, "God, I thank You that I am not like other men—extortioners, unjust, adulterers, or even as this tax collector. I fast twice a week; I give tithes of all that I possess.' And the tax collector, standing afar off, would not so much as raise his eyes to heaven, but beat his breast, saying, "God, be merciful to me a sinner!' I tell you, this man went down to his house justified rather than the other…"*

> —Luke 18:10-14

Although the situation described by Jesus in this parable is different from the experience of war, the main idea reveals that in many cases in life we are so overwhelmed by grief or sorrow or guilt that we really don't have the words to say when we go before God. In this case the Pharisee had the fancy words and all the right things to say, but his heart was not right. He was puffed up and arrogant.

The second man, a tax collector, was so ashamed of himself he could not even look up towards God. The situation in his life was overwhelming, and he could not muster the words that were no doubt ready to burst forth from his heart.

It is the times when we are humble and realize there are things so much bigger than we are that God steps in and takes over. Therefore, I know God heard my prayers because the Holy Spirit spoke them to Him.

Regardless of your theological perspective on this particular topic, there can be no doubt that we have all felt this way at one point or another in our lives. Perhaps we are dealing with the death of a loved one or the sudden news of a terminal illness or maybe the complete hopelessness of a spouse who has walked out or maybe a child who is far from God and doing horrible, even dangerous things.

Sometimes, as was the case with the tax collector, it is overwhelming guilt that weighs us down to the point of being speechless before God. All of us have been at a point in life where there simply are not words for the pain we feel. This was where I found myself over and over again as I prayed for our guys.

One thing that really strengthened me during this time was the unbelievable outpouring of prayers and support from back home in the states. To this day I am amazed at how many emails, letters, and packages I received telling me that people were praying daily for me and our guys.

A few months into my deployment I linked up with a gentleman, Phil Presley, back home who received one of my weekly email updates that had been forwarded to him. Phil became a source of amazing support and strength through this time, as he was the organizer of a huge worldwide prayer chain that was praying for the military.

I began to send prayer requests to him for our wounded and for some of the things that were happening. He immediately activated his prayer chain which I came to find out later was going to more than 20,000 people worldwide!

The flood of email that came in response to his prayer request sent out on my behalf was almost too numerous to read. Sometimes it would take me several hours to read each one that came in, each with strong prayers and words of encouragement. I can tell you that this was one of the biggest things that kept me going during my time in Iraq.

Throughout my time in Ramadi, the prayers and emails poured in. Never was this more vital than during the battle for Fallujah, Operation Phantom Fury, from 8 to 14 November. This was the much anticipated battle to take the city of Fallujah back from the estimated three to five thousand insurgents who had laid siege to the town of 350,000 people.

In April, 2004, we had advanced with 2,000 troops only to stop because of the outcry against civilian casualties. The planning for this second offensive had been going on since that time but intensified in the three weeks leading up to 8 November. Not only were there plans from a military perspective, but we were making plans as well for the expected increase in casualties.

This operation would see some 10,000 of our troops on the ground with another 2,000 Iraqi Army troops. We knew that our normal daily load of wounded would increase four to five times and that medical facilities would be overwhelmed.

Together with the medical chain of command that included the 1st Marine Expeditionary Force's Surgeon as well as the medical personnel from all the subordinate units, we began to put into place a plan to accommodate what we expected to be very heavy casualties.

Weeks and weeks of logistical, preparatory work was done. Supplies were beefed up at each facility. More personnel were brought in from other parts of the country to augment and increase each facility's capacity and ability to do life saving surgery.

More helicopter casualty evacuation teams were positioned close to Fallujah. Extensive detailed plans were made for the commencement of the operation that would begin at the close of Ramadan.

Although everything possible was done to prepare us all for what would certainly be one of the fiercest battles since Vietnam, nothing could have prepared us for the reality of what we would face. On the Patient Evacuation Team we beefed up our crew to two people per 12-hour shift with an additional phone line installed to help accommodate the increased number of calls.

On the first two days of the offensive our casualty rate did go up quite a bit, but it was still manageable. We were seeing 50 to 60 wounded each day. We managed to get most of them from the point of injury to an operating table in less than an hour. On the battlefield, this is critical for survival.

We in the medical community refer to this as the "Golden Hour." This comes from research that was done after Vietnam which showed that the greatest chance of survival for those who have sustained penetrating trauma on the battlefield such as gunshot wounds or shrapnel stand the greatest chance of survival when they are able to get to an operating room with a surgeon within one hour.

We religiously adhered to this principle and were able to get most to the OR in less than an hour. By the end of the second day we were exhausted but holding our own and getting the wounded where they needed to go quickly. My journal entry for 8 November:

"The attack in Fallujah officially began last night; however, we didn't push forward until today at 7 p.m. I am blessed beyond belief at the lack of casualties so far—only two have been killed in action and 12 wounded which is not good, but is FAR fewer than I had anticipated. The prayers of everyone back home are working miracles today.

My devotion for today is from the third Psalm. Wow, how completely applicable it is to what is going on. It speaks to our situation and to my individual fears as well. God is a shield all around me. He gives me rest and breaks the enemy to pieces. This is truly the working of the Holy Spirit to bring this encouragement to my heart on this day. There are many more days to come, but the Lord is the Lord over all," as Psalm 3 reminds us:

> *"O LORD, how many are my foes! How many rise up against me! Many are saying of me, "God will not deliver him." But you are a shield around me, O LORD; you bestow glory on me and lift up my head. To the LORD I cry aloud, and he answers me from his holy hill. I lie down and sleep; I wake again, because the LORD sustains me. I will not fear the tens of thousands drawn up against me on every side. Arise, O LORD! Deliver me, O my God! Strike all my enemies on the jaw; break the teeth of the wicked. From the LORD comes deliverance. May your blessing be on your people."*

When the third day began all hell broke loose on the battlefield, and we began to have so many casualties that every medical facility including the Army hospitals in Baghdad and Balad were over capacity with waiting times in the OR's.

Sometimes there was as much as eight to nine hours waiting time before wounded could get to a surgeon. Calls were coming in so rapidly that we had all four helicopter CASEVAC sections running around the clock to move people. We had five and six calls coming in at the same time.

By the end of the third day we had moved more than 100 wounded in less than 24 hours. We were well over 200 casualties total for the operation with some 20 killed in action. The load was taking a toll on me physically, emotionally and spiritually.

One of the worst parts was there was no down time to unwind. A 12 hour shift doing this type of work is actually more like 13 to 14 hours because you have to turn over with the next crew. If things were hot and heavy, which most of the time they were, you would not be able to complete a turnover for an hour or more. This made coping extremely difficult.

It was certainly only by the grace of God and time in prayer and the Word that would carry me through this ordeal. It seemed that an encouraging email from someone back home would always come through at just the right time to lift my spirits. God's timing is always impeccable and perfect.

As time was coming to an end for Operation Phantom Fury, we were able to finally breathe, and little by little we were able to evacuate all the casualties off the battlefield and into Germany and back home.

During the course of praying for all the wounded and communicating with those back home on the prayer chain, we began to see answers to our prayers. Those who had life-threatening wounds and conditions that should have taken their lives were making full recoveries.

The prayer team members at home were beginning to link up with the Marines and Sailors who were arriving at the Naval Hospital in Camp Pendleton. They had the opportunity to tell them about all the people praying for them. They also came to find out that the one who was coordinating their medical evacuation was also praying for them the whole time.

So many of those who were wounded, as well as their families, were able to be comforted and ministered to with this knowledge. The prayer team also was able to lead a number of them to Christ right there in the hospital.

In addition to this, we were able to communicate messages from the Marines in the hospital to the front line hospital corpsman on the battlefield who had saved their lives when they were hit. The corpsmen who received these messages were very happy to hear that their Marines were going to be OK.

I was blessed to be able to pass these messages on to the "docs" as we don't always get a chance to hear back from those we serve. Many times a person gets evacuated to a hospital and then back home, and we never hear how they are doing. I know God orchestrated these messages to encourage and strengthen those on the battlefield still doing their job. God's ability to get a message to whomever He chooses is beyond our comprehension sometimes.

As Fallujah came to somewhat of a conclusion our casualty rates slowed back down to the point they were prior to the operation. As the holidays came upon us, we enjoyed a time of relative calm and quiet with very few serious injuries.

It was as though God allowed our guys to have a bit of a break to rest and catch their breath after the hellish battle that claimed 51 lives and saw more than 425 wounded. It was during this time that I was able to collect my thoughts and reflect on how amazing God's grace and protection were during this historic time.

What could have been far worse ended with a military victory in six short days and amounted to a spiritual victory for so many.

During the holidays, I experienced a bout of homesickness that I was not ready for. Although God's Holy Spirit was sustaining me spiritually, my heart was breaking inside being away from Kellee and Cameron as well as my extended Generations church family.

As I battled through day after day of holiday time, I was more and more aware of my strong desire to be home. God began to minister to me with the knowledge that He had placed me here at this time to show His love to those who were with me.

They too had the same feelings, and His plan for me was to extend His love to them through our Bible studies and through our work. I was comforted by knowing that there was a divine reason why I was away from home. It was His plan from the beginning that I be there for His purposes. I allowed God to strengthen me and went about His business ministering His Word to the people.

Throughout this time I conducted weekly Bible studies to a core group of 10 to 15 people. During our studies through James' Epistle and later through Paul's letter to the Galatians, many were encouraged in their faith and stirred to live right for God.

His Word was penetrating our hearts in a new way and people were finding the strength in Christ they needed to not only get through the deployment but also to go back home in victory.

One young man accepted the Lord during one of the Galatians studies after hearing about the story of a bondservant. Paul describes himself as in chains for Christ and as a bondservant by choice. When this story was unfolded to him, the Holy Spirit tugged his heart, and he accepted the invitation to spend eternity in the Master's house.

"For do I now persuade men, or God? Or do I seek to please men? For if I still pleased men, I would not be a bondservant of Christ."
—Galatians 1:12

"Paul, a bondservant of Jesus Christ, called to be an apostle, separated to the gospel of God."

The incredible picture of a slave or servant entering into a different kind of relationship with the Master is so wonderful, and I've never heard it captured better than in the following story by Trish Harrison:

In those days, many had to seek work as hired servants for wealthy landowners. I was a poor peasant girl. I needed to find work and to be taken care of. Word spread throughout the village of one wealthy landowner who was very hard to work for but was fair and good to his servants. He always treated them well and didn't abuse them. The work was hard but he took good care of his servants as long as they were good workers. Those who slacked off were sent away without any further compensation. I came upon the stately mansion.

It was the most awesome mansion I had ever seen! As far as the eye could see were the vast fields, vineyards, and livestock. I was excited yet very much afraid to enter those gates. Many spoke of the owner's son. He was a very firm taskmaster but also kind, gentle and understanding. He required that when you work for him it was for a total of seven years. After that time, you were set free with a very handsome settlement in which you could take care of yourself for quite sometime!

I entered the gates, trembling. I was brought to the owner's son. He was very specific what he expected from me, but in turn, he would treat me fairly and pay me a just wage. My work began in the fields. We would put in a very long, hard day but at the end of the day, he would feed us a very good meal and our quarters were very comfortable compared to most servants' camps. Once in a while, the owner's son would walk among the fields just to check on us. Those of us who were working hard were encouraged.

Those who were not working hard were warned and then later sent away if their work did not improve.

At the end of the seven years, each servant was given a graduation ceremony of sorts. There would be a special party where the master's son would congratulate them and give them a total of $15,000 compensation to help them along the way. They were set free and on their own. Although the subject rarely came up, all servants were given a chance at that time to become the master's bondservants—servants for life—completely sold out to the master, never to be free. In turn, the master would take care of them for the rest of their lives. Very few even considered this kind of servitude.

As the end of my seven years approached, I asked many of the other servants if they had ever considered becoming a bondservant.

They laughed and said, "No way! Only a crazy person would even consider something like that!"

Once in a while I would see one of the owner's bondservants. They were different. They would come out to the fields to bring a message from the master, but they didn't mingle among us.

Every time the master's son would come to the field, my heart would leap for joy! He was such a kind, gentle person, yet strong and unwavering. He was a very powerful man—much like his father. At times when I would see him, it would almost take my breath away. My heart would beat faster and faster and I would cling to his every word, although he rarely spoke directly to me.

One time, he stopped and asked me my name. I told him that I really didn't have a name. He just smiled. It was time for my "graduation." I was being set free that night.

The master's son called me up and congratulated me on a fine job. He was about to give me my compensation when I said in a very low voice,

"I don't want to leave—I want to be your bondservant."

The crowd of servants gasped! He silenced them and asked me to repeat myself. I said,

"I don't want to leave you master. I want to stay with you forever. I want to be your bondservant!"

He asked me if I had any idea what kind of decision I was making. I told him I did, but he asked me to think about it overnight and let him know in the morning.

When the morning came, he approached me again,

"Have you made your decision?"

I said, "Yes, my lord. I want to be your bondservant."

He smiled and escorted me to a block of wood. He told me to lie down. The block of wood was put behind my left ear. One of the other bondservants took a nail and pounded it into my earlobe to make a hole. He inserted an earring of fine gold. This was the seal of our commitment. The pain in my ear was very intense but the joy in my heart was overwhelming.

As I began to leave, the master's son called me over to him. He comforted me in my pain and told me to pack my bags.

I said, "But master, where am I going?"

He told me that I would no longer live in the servant's camp, but would live in the master's house. I was his property now and he would always take care of me—no matter what! He even gave me a name!

The mansion was more awesome than I could ever imagine. I even had my own room! I still worked very hard for the master and his son, but the atmosphere was so different. I lived in his house. I began to know every intimate detail of his life. I saw exactly how he lived.

Every once in a while he would come to my room and just chat with me. I waited on him hand and foot and took care of his every need. I began to know exactly what he liked and what he didn't like.

As the years passed by, I became very old and feeble. One day while I was taking a message for him to the field, I felt faint. I had to sit down. The master's son rushed out to check on me. He took one look at me and picked me up in his arms and carried me back to his father's house. He put me in my bed and waited on me hand and foot. He wouldn't let me lift a finger. I asked him why he was doing this and he replied,

"I made a commitment to you years ago that if you became my bondservant, I would take care of you for the rest of your life, even when you are old and feeble. It is now my turn to wait on you!"

I have never regretted the day I made the decision to become his bondservant. I know that no matter what happens, he will be there for me. And this earring of fine gold never fails to remind me of that relationship.

I always wondered about the other servants—how long did their money last? And what ever became of them when they were old? Who took care of them when they could no longer take care of themselves?

"Henceforth I call you not servants; for the servant knoweth not what his lord doeth: but I have called you friends; for all things that I have heard of my Father, I have made known unto you."

—John 15:15

Trish Harrison

*   *   *

The beautiful expression of God's love to those who submit their lives to His purpose is beyond description. His love is without limits and knows no boundaries. We are transformed from slaves to sons and daughters of God.

While I was in Iraq during my second deployment, I often wondered why my purpose was so different from the first time, when I had experienced so much ministry and first-hand revival. God taught me about the church and how He works. Knowing I would be there longer this time, I assumed that the revival would be even greater.

What I found, however, is that the revival was not in those around me but in my own heart! God taught me a greater personal lesson this time around in the areas of self-control and diligence, as well as the lesson of perseverance in times of trouble and separation from family.

This was a time where I rested from my very busy schedule of ministry back home and focused on being still and knowing that He is God—a time where He spoke so clearly to my heart and taught me to be an intercessor for His Kingdom. I had to learn that He is the One I can trust and lean on in any circumstance, especially when I feel absolutely helpless.

Out of this time came the reflections that fill the rest of this book—deep insights into the life that God desires to shape through trial and adversity on life's battlefield.

In many ways this second time has taught me more about walking in intimacy and complete dependence on Him than when I was in Kuwait. This was the "behind the scenes" view on the outward expression of revival and ministry that I experienced in Kuwait.

It was as though God were saying, "This is what the Kingdom of God is all about. This is how I want ministry to be. Now, let me take your life and mold it into the vessel that I will use to accomplish this kind of ministry always."

As my time was coming to an end on my second tour, I thought that perhaps I would have the opportunity to wind down a bit from the craziness of the last six months. This was where I was wrong!

The last couple of weeks in my job as Patient Evacuation Coordinator saw some of the most intense fighting in the entire 22 months since the conflict in Iraq began. Truly, we had experienced a living hell during Operation Phantom

Fury in Fallujah, but we were able to maintain and make it through with a relatively strong victory militarily on the battlefield.

The last week in January saw two major events which continued to test my resolve and that of all the military. The first of these was on 26 January when we suffered the worst single day since the beginning of the war.

It started on my shift at 0145 when we got a call that a helicopter had gone down out in the western part of the country. We had dealt with a number of downed aircraft in the previous five months, two of which were in one day during the Fallujah operation. In all the incidents there were bad injuries, and some had died. We knew this one would not be good.

We were not prepared for the reality of what would prove to be the worst loss of life in any single day. It turned out the chopper was a CH-53E, which is the largest of the helicopters used in the military aircraft arsenal. When word started coming in we realized the aircraft had been fully combat loaded with Infantry Marines and a full crew of four. That amounted to 31 total on board.

We were hopeful that there would be minor injuries and that we would be able to treat everyone and get them back to their unit.

The first call came in with an initial report of 18 dead. The silence in the command center was sobering. By the time the rest of the news came in our worst fears had been confirmed: there were no survivors. This was more than most of us could handle, and no one really talked except when we had to in order to do our job.

Soon afterward we received another call that an ambush had taken place near the Haditha Dam to the north. Nine Marines were involved in this attack, and two were already confirmed to have been killed in action. I worked feverishly to move the remaining seven wounded Marines, but in the end, two more died as a result of their injuries.

In another place on the battlefield a soldier had been killed in an attack. All in all, 36 lost their lives that night which eclipsed the 31 who had been killed on 23 March 2003 during the first few days of the ground war. Most of those had occurred near An Nasariya in the battle that resulted with the soldiers from the 507th Maintenance Company becoming prisoners of war—including Jessica Lynch.

To make matters worse, the elections were quickly approaching, and there were great preparations being made throughout Iraq to make the balloting locations safe for the voters and to shield them from the certain attacks by the insurgents.

There were video and audio messages daily from different groups warning voters not to take part in the elections and threatening wide-spread violence. Fresh off the events of the 26th all of us were highly tense and stressed.

Many of us were praying and fasting for days before the elections for the safety of not only our troops but the Iraqi people. In fact, the Navy's Chief of Chaplains sent out an email several days before the election to all Navy Chaplains to pray and fast corporately as a body for God's hand of protection to be upon the whole process that day.

When the day came we waited in anticipation. We waited, and we waited. Not one casualty in our area of Iraq was reported all day. In fact, we had fewer patients that day than any other day prior to it!

A total of three routine patients were moved by us for appointments. We were all jubilant at this obvious answer to our prayers and even more so finding out the next day that the voter turnout throughout the country defied the insurgent's threats and exceeded the most optimistic expectations.

The news footage from around the country showed scores of people in the street celebrating, dancing and singing. They had exercised their freedom to make their voices heard and had done so with a resounding shout.

This sense of joy and excitement as well as the tremendous emotion felt by so many Iraqis was later echoed in President Bush's State of the Union speech on 2 February 2005, when he introduced Safia Taleb al-Suhail, an Iraqi human rights advocate who had voted on Election Day.

Her father, an Iraqi political leader, had been killed by Saddam Hussein's henchmen in the mid 90's. The camera panned to her holding her two fingers up in the "V" sign with her blue ink still present on her voting finger. She fought to hold back tears as she received a standing ovation from lawmakers.

The President also introduced Bill and Janet Norwood who were seated directly in front of Ms. al-Suhail. Their son Byron, a Marine sergeant, died fighting in Fallujah several months prior to the elections. The scene was emotionally peaked as Ms. al-Suhail and Janet Norwood embraced, both shaking as they wept.

The gratitude of those liberated showed no boundaries as she thanked the one who had paid the price with the blood of her own son. This exchange drew the longest round of applause all night and visibly moved the President. It moved everyone who saw it.

For me, just knowing that we were part of this history, that we were the ones who stood the watch that day to provide the protection for the people, that we were the ones who had by and large made this possible caused us to walk a little taller.

You realize at those moments that you have been part of something so much bigger than yourself—something so historically significant.

Chapter 4

The Double-STP

*"You are of God, little children, and have overcome
them, because He who is in you is greater than he who
is in the world."*

—1 John 4:4

On 1 February, I found myself on a CH-46 helicopter
being whisked back to Al Taqaddum in preparation for my
departure some weeks later. I had not had a day off in
nearly six months and was so ready to rest and have a few
days when I didn't need to be somewhere at a certain time.

It gave me an opportunity to "defragment" the hard
drive in my head and to have some extended prayer and
meditation time in God's Word. During this time I also had
the opportunity to go to one of the medical facilities that we
had frequently sent patients to during my time as the patient
evacuation coordinator. I knew many of my staff from before, and I thanked them for the tremendous work they had
done.

I could not even imagine having to deal with some of
the things they had to encounter during their six-month
tour. Their unit saw more than 1000 patients with nearly
40% of them needing surgery.

In fact, on one particular day in November while Operation Phantom Fury was going on in Fallujah, this unit,
the SSTP, received 43 patients. That particular day we had
moved a total of 107 patients throughout the battle space,
and they bore a large chunk of those wounded.

They all showed such composure and professionalism. I was told they didn't think about how many patients were coming in, they just kept working.

In my role as patient evacuation coordinator I had begun the practice of earnestly and diligently praying for each and every casualty as soon as the call came into the Command Operations Center. From the moment I received the call until they were out of the woods, I and many others would pray for them.

One of the hallmarks of my prayers when dealing with the wounded was that God would supernaturally work through the hands of the medical personnel handling the case—specifically, that He would work through the surgeon's hands to heal and touch each person.

In my last few weeks in Iraq, I spent some time with a number of these surgeons, doctors, nurses, and corpsmen who had been on the receiving end of so many of my calls. The aspect of my prayer that asked for God to use and work through the surgeons as they operated on each patient took on a whole new meaning to me as I spoke to them about their reflections of those moments.

Lowell Chambers

The first person I spoke with was Lieutenant Commander Lowell Chambers, a Navy general surgeon based out of Camp Pendleton Naval Hospital. The first thing that grabbed me about Dr. Chambers was his passion for what he does and his obvious love for His Lord.

As he began to recall some of the more memorable moments from the last six months, it became clear to me that being a surgeon was not a profession to him, it was his ministry. This is what God called him to do. Knowing the prayers I had been offering to God as I moved patients to this facility were directly answered through people like Dr.

Chambers began to give me a strong sense of the providence of God.

God's purposes and His fingerprints were all over every aspect of the casualty process. He had strategically placed faithful believers in every part of the process to intercede and provide the touch of healing to each person as he or she experienced the pains of physical wounds and the nightmarish experiences from the battlefield.

Dr. Chambers began to describe for me some of the moments that had most impacted him during this time. He related one such story that really grabbed my heart and spoke volumes to me about the love of God showing through this man.

An Army captain by the name of Daniel Gade who came into the SSTP. This is the facility Dr. Chambers works in that is a combination of a FRSS or Forward Resuscitative Surgical System and a STP or Shock Trauma Platoon. When put together they formed the Double-STP.

Captain Gade had been near Ramadi with his unit when an Improvised Explosive Device with 155mm artillery shells blew up under his vehicle and severely wounded him, severing all of his femoral vessels.

My team at the patient Evacuation Team received the call for Captain Gade on 10 January 2005 at 1552 in the afternoon and immediately began to pray for him. We loaded him up in Ramadi on a chopper and transported him to the SSTP at Al Taqaddum. He arrived at 1620, some 40 minutes after the incident.

Dr. Chambers described the extent of the injuries and the contamination to Captain Gade's leg as profound and among the worst dealt with by the SSTP team during their tour. The SSTP team initially labored to resuscitate Captain Gade from severe hemorrhagic shock utilizing multiple units of blood, including 14 units donated on the spot by fellow warriors.

Daniel was in the OR for nearly nine hours with the entire surgical team working feverishly to control multiple bleeding sites from his severely injured leg and to restore blood flow through small bypasses they placed in the leg.

This ordeal was mentally and physically exhausting for the team, but there was something profoundly different about Captain Daniel Gade. Dr. Chambers felt a unique bond with this man for reasons he didn't know at the time.

After hours of surgery, the team had done all they could do. As a matter of fact, Dr. Chambers said, "My surgical skills, while good, were completely inadequate to handle this case and many others that ultimately had favorable outcomes."

It was kind of funny that when Doc Chambers told me this, I couldn't help but think of a scene from a movie I had seen many years ago where there was a thoracic heart surgeon who was accused in a lawsuit of having a "God complex." His complex was because he felt he was in the place of God to make life and death decisions.

As Doc Chambers spoke to me I couldn't help but see symbolism in this. While the other doctor had a "God Complex" which focused on himself, Dr. Chambers had a "God Complex" that was rightly related to God. He was not in the place of God, but rather used by God who worked through him to touch people on the OR table.

His skills, wisdom and professionalism were all a result of the gifts given by God to a man who would humbly employ them while giving God all the glory for the results. What an amazing and refreshing quality to see in such a great surgeon and man!

Prior to the MEDEVAC, which would take Daniel to the next level of care in Baghdad, this humble surgeon who had worked so hard on his patient laid his head on the side of Daniel Gade and wept and prayed for him.

His prayers were that of surrender and deep concern not only for Daniel but for his family. He lifted his spirit up to God realizing that there was nothing more he could do. "Please Lord, don't let him die."

Later, Dr. Chambers realized that Daniel Gade was a strong believer in Jesus and that the bond he had felt was the bond of the Holy Spirit who was in them both. God had given him a special burden for this guy forging a sacred bond of Christian love despite the fact that before this moment they had never met.

He told me about a website that was following the progress of Daniel's recovery at Walter Reed Medical Center in Washington, D.C. The prayers and outpouring of support found for Daniel and his family from all over the country made a profound impression on Dr. Chambers as he has had a renewed faith in the goodness of Americans. (www2.caringbridge.org/dc/danielgade/).

Through reading the loving and compassionate responses from people all over the nation for Daniel and his family, Dr. Chambers saw a side of America that he at one point doubted still existed.

From the site I was able to gather some information on why it was that this Navy doctor had felt such a bond of love for this Army captain on that day. From a prayer card written prior to deploying to Iraq, Daniel wrote:

Dear Prayer Warriors,

My unit and I were recently alerted for deployment from Korea to Iraq to participate in Operation Iraqi Freedom. We will serve this mission for the next year. During this time my soldiers and I will face grave danger each step of the way, and our families will face a year without their husbands, fathers, and sons.

My wife Wendy and I believe firmly that God's purpose is being served by this unexpected detour in our lives—there are too many obvious indicators of Him acting directly in this situation for there to be any doubt. Because there is no doubt, we will resolutely face our next, difficult steps with our heads held high and set our feet upon the path He has provided.

The most important thing you can provide during this journey is your companionship through prayer. Please allow this prayer card to assist you as you pray for us. We believe strongly that your prayers will have a dramatic impact on lives and this situation.

Thank you for standing with us in prayer during this challenge-filled time. Again, we are confident that God's path is clear for us and that we are following His direction in our lives. Jeremiah 29:11 says, "For I know the plans I have for you," declares the Lord, "plans to prosper you and not to harm you, plans to give you hope and a future."

God bless you,
Daniel Gade

*   *   *

From Dr. Chambers' account of his experience in the operating room with Daniel, the bond that he so strongly felt with this man, and the tears he wept at Daniel's side as he prayed confirmed in my spirit that God had answered my prayers more specifically than I could have ever imagined. Not only had He worked through the hands of this doctor and man of God, but He had also used him to pray for his patient during the procedure, afterwards and even to this day.

The bond that God forged between Dr. Lowell Chambers and Captain Daniel Gade will endure forever and always be a defining moment in both their lives.

I asked Dr. Chambers how he dealt on a daily basis with such horrible situations that don't always turn out for the best. Early in his life, he enlisted in the Marine Corps and served during Desert Storm as a Lance Corporal with BSSG-5, 1st Military Police Company.

It was this experience that gave him this unique bond and ability to identify with Marines and Soldiers now as a surgeon. Additionally, he spends time after each day and each procedure praying and reading God's Word. He spends time in reflection and prayerful meditation, always wanting to improve upon the next OR experience, always pushing himself to do better for these guys.

My impression after speaking to him was that this was every bit as effective a ministry as any pastor or teacher. He has left an enduring mark on so many people he has touched, a touch that has forever changed their lives. After talking with Dr. Chambers he asked if we could close in prayer which made my heart leap inside my chest.

He lead us in prayer and afterward I left the operating room where the interview had taken place with a unique sense of awe at having just seen a part of God's mystery revealed to me. I was truly thankful for the opportunity I had to talk with this wonderful man of God.

Gini Hinrichs

Another person I talked to was a Navy nurse by the name of Gini Hinrichs. At the young age of 23, she grew up more in the last six months than she had ever thought possible.

In talking with her I was curious to gain her perspective on the things she had experienced and those episodes that had most dramatically left their mark upon her life. She related to me that prior to coming to Iraq, and even on the plane ride from the states, she never feared for her life.

Although she had grown up in a Lutheran home and attended church for most of her life, she found that she never really "got it" until coming to Iraq. She had always been extremely independent and had even criticized one of her roommates in college who would always pray before making decisions. This frustrated her because she reasoned that "any strong person should be able to just make a decision." This would all change for Gini during her tour in Iraq.

One of the most decisive moments for Ensign Hinrichs came soon after arriving in the country with the realization that she was not in control. There were so many things happening around her that she had no ability to affect or to change. At first, this gave her a real sense of fear, especially when there were rockets and mortars coming close to where she was.

In fact, she recalled one moment while they were working on a patient in the OR when rockets started impacting close to the SSTP. Each one landed a little closer than the last one had. The operating team was now on the floor working on their patient. She recalls that at that moment she was very scared and very sure that the next rocket was going to hit her tent.

One thing that really impacted her was seeing the faith of Chief Petty Officer Suzy Dugger. Suzy would walk with her head held high and despite the danger showed no fear. Gini wondered what was different about Suzy and said to herself, "I need to have what she has."

When she asked the Chief what it was about her that was so different, Suzy replied immediately, "I am secure in God, and I know exactly where I am going if I die."

From that point on Gini picked up her Bible and began to make Christ a living and real part of her life. She now says that she walks in confidence knowing that nothing will happen that God does not allow, and if something does happen to her, it is her time to be with Him.

Gini recalled for me one of the defining moments for her while in Iraq. She had an entire family of Iraqi's come in who had been shot up after running a road block. A number of the kids had been killed in the incident, and there was a four year old little girl who had a severe wound to the face.

As she was relating this story to me she teared up with the memory. They had worked so hard to do all they could for her. She remembered feeling such a sense of helplessness. She found herself praying the whole time for this little child as the surgeons worked to save her.

Outside the OR, she took turns holding the brother of the little girl. He held on to her trembling with fear at what had happened. She could not get the face of this little girl out of her head and again had to let go and give this to God.

She found herself in her own ability unable to deal with such an emotional and traumatic experience, but when she surrendered this to Christ, she received a feeling of complete peace and rest.

Gini related many such stories to me about times that she was unable to do anything except pray. The circumstances of this war were often beyond her ability to cope.

She recalled another incident while flying on the MEDEVAC helicopter with a critical patient who had a head injury. The team had done all that was humanly possible to save him, and she found herself at one moment during the flight laying her head on his shoulder and praying for him. She asked God to please hold him up and save his life.

At 23 years of age, this young nurse had experienced more life than most people twice her age. She credited her experiences in Iraq with deepening her faith and developing an intimacy with Jesus that she had never known before.

She told me "It's OK to have faith in people, but you have to know they will let you down at some time—God is the only one who will never let you down. When you come into an environment like this you are going to see things and experience things that you can't even imagine and the only way to get through is with that close relationship with God."

God in His great mercy and providence used this young nurse to impact many and, as an instrument in His hand, to touch each person with His love. I asked her who has impacted her the most while here—who will she never forget?

Again with tears in her eyes she closed with, "Some of the kids—I will never forget the kids." Life is too short to not know where you stand or where you will go should your day come. Ensign Gini Hinrichs was yet another example of the hand of God working in this place called the battlefield.

Suzy Dugger

Known by most of the SSTP staff as the "Mother Hen," 42 year old Chief Petty Officer Suzy Dugger served as the Leading Chief Petty Officer for the Forward Resuscitative Surgical System-1 (FRSS-1) during the time I was in Iraq.

Her responsibility with this unit, while serving as an Independent Duty Corpsman, was to assist in the emergency resuscitation of patients as well as to provide leadership and to mentor junior enlisted sailors and junior officers. Although this is her official capacity, it is not why people of every rank find themselves drawn to her for her guidance and insight.

Her personality is outgoing and warm with a strange combination of rough edges and off-the-wall humor. She said sometimes she feels like the grungy old Gunnery Sergeant immortalized in so many of Hollywood's war movies.

An odd mishmash of strength and composure under intense pressure and danger with an uncommon approachability and compassion for every person she meets are just some of the refreshing qualities that give Suzy her mom-like appeal.

I have a bit of history with Suzy as we both made Chief Petty Officer at the same time, going through the famed Chief's initiation and academy together with 39 other chief selectees from the Camp Pendleton area.

The Chief Petty Officer's Mess is a time honored fraternity, rich in naval customs and traditions and unmatched brotherhood in a secular organization. All 39 of us will never forget our experiences together, and we will share a bond for life.

Making Chief is the benchmark for any enlisted Sailor in the Navy and when you finally get your Anchors pinned on your collar, you suddenly realize why. Outside my relationships with those in the Body of Christ, nothing rivals the Chief Petty Officer family.

People agreed that Suzy was the common denominator for many of the team members. I shared this with her as we sat down to talk about her experiences. This fact seemed to be somewhat overwhelming to her as she wasn't really sure why. She suspected it had to do with her personality, but I suggested it might have had more to do with something a little deeper than that.

She then shared with me that when September 11 happened she came to the startling realization that our nation was now at war and as an Independent Duty Corpsman she knew this meant one thing—deployment to the combat zone.

As she wrestled with this fact, an overwhelming bout of anxiety affected her ability to be courageous and composed. She said one day she got down on her knees and prayed a very specific prayer that God would give her peace and take away her anxieties about what she knew was certainly on her horizon.

After this definitive moment, she said that God took away all her anxiety, and the feelings had not returned. When she found herself in Iraq for the second time her composure and conduct were something that gave strength to everyone around her. "I know that I am coming home. I know that nothing will happen to me unless God allows it to happen."

This strong assurance of where she stands in Christ has given her strength beyond strength to walk with confidence and to hold her head high despite the very real dangers of the combat zone.

Suzy told me about one of her patients that she called her "cry patient." This struck me as curious, and then she told me that everyone of the staff members has at least one "cry patient." This is a specific patient that makes you cry for some reason or another.

This particular patient arrived in serious condition with a very weak pulse. The extent of the injuries were so severe that it was questionable as to weather he would be able to survive. As the team worked hard to save his life and stabilize him, a few more urgent patients came in with injuries not considered to be as potentially mortal.

On the battlefield, there is a precedent for triage and sorting of casualties according to priority which is slightly different than in civilian medicine. You want to save as many as possible who can return to the battlefield to continue the fight. If there are multiple patients who are severe but one is going to require extensive surgery, time and resources to save, the policy is to divert the attention to those patients who require less time to stabilize and save.

Said another way, a patient who may require six hours of surgery to stabilize and even then will probably die could be set aside to work on say three patients who only require two hours of surgery and have a greater chance of survival. Suzy's "cry patient" was one of these who had to be set aside to accommodate the greater good.

When the decision was made by the team to work on the other patients rather than this guy it absolutely ripped her heart from her chest. To make things worse, she had a number of brand new corpsmen who had never really been exposed to this kind of life or death decision—she worried about their mental health.

She had to make a very difficult decision to shield these young Sailors from any more exposure; so, she took on the emotional task of "packaging" this young man who had died to prepare him for his final flight home.

As she moved him on the gurney, his left hand fell out of the blanket exposing his wedding band. Imagining the Marines in dress blues knocking on the door of his house to tell his wife drove Chief Hospital Corpsman Suzy Dugger to her knees in one of the empty wards.

She often found herself there during her time in the combat zone crying out to God, making it clear to her Creator that she could not shoulder this responsibility; it was too much for her. Each time God would faithfully take the cup from her and restore her peace so she could face another day, another hour, another minute—to be ready when the next patient darkened the door of the SSTP.

Suzy wrote home several days later recalling these moments:

"1245, Friday 24 Sep, the first group of CPOs showed up on my door step. They were all going to meet here at my workspace and then we were going to head out to a meeting, but I never made it over there. The call came in over the radio at 1250, "Five incoming wounded, two urgent surgical and two urgent." We weren't sure what that meant but we knew it didn't sound good.

As the patients arrived they brought the first one in and put him on the OR table, the doctors were frantic; he stopped breathing and lost his pulse on the bird; they were doing CPR and trying to find his wound. His pupils were fixed and dilated. He had blood on him but we couldn't find a wound. They rolled him over and found a single gun shot or fragment wound to the back of his head. We had another patient over on the other OR table and I can't remember what his injuries were because there had been so many that I'm getting them confused. I only know that the Doctors worked on the one guy for about 15 min and then had to pronounce him dead because we had another patient waiting to get on the table.

I assisted in taking what we call our "Fallen Angel" off the table; we had him covered in a wool blanket, and I was directing the other stretcher bearers to put him in Ward two because all of the Chiefs who had arrived for the meeting were in Ward four, directly across from where we were placing our patients. As we carried him to the ward, his arm fell out from underneath the blanket; there on his blood stained hand was a gold wedding band. I immediately teared up. My thoughts went out to his young bride, and I wondered if they had any children. I later found out he had onc toddler and one on the way.

Once we got him into the expectant tent, I dismissed all the stretcher bearers so they could help out with other patients and I started to prepare the body for the mortuary affairs personnel. I took off his ring and watch and put it in a bag that had the rest of his blood stained clothes. I then fell to my knees beside the cot and held the young man's hand and started to pray for his soul and his family. It was then that the Chaplain came in. He prayed with me and I then wiped the tears from my eyes and got my composure before I walked out. I had too many people out there that were counting on me to keep it together, not to mention, all my Chief peers were in the tent across the way."

*   *   *

This is a side that Suzy seldom revealed to anyone else, but none the less, a side that was as real as the confident and courageous Chief Petty Officer that everyone else knew and looked to for strength.

In her words: "I could not have made it through these last two deployments without my faith in Christ. He has been my mainstay and my sure thing in every situation. My relationship with Him has become so much closer during this time. I have come to realize that I could never have made it through this after seeing the things I have seen, apart from my faith in Him."

Suzy became very transparent and vulnerable with me, sharing that many times she doesn't feel that she is worthy of God's love because of many of the things she has done in her life. I asked her how she thought God felt about her now.

"I know that He loves me. I think He sometimes says, 'Suzy, what are you doing?' But I know that He loves me. No problem, no worry, no fear, is too great for God. No matter what you are going through you've got to share it with Him, He's got to be your best friend. You go home at night and you talk about your day with your husband, wife, or your neighbor; why can't you do that with God? If you can lay it all out before Him, you will start to have the relationship with God that you should have."

At the end of our interview I looked at Suzy and let her know that she was certainly worthy of God's love. After all, He had died for her. With a hug and some tears, we concluded our time together.

Tina Terrones

I've known Hospital Corpsman Third Class Tina Terrones for nearly five years, having served with her at Medical Logistics Company at Camp Pendleton in 2000 and 2001.

During my one-and-a-half years there I had the amazing blessing of seeing many of my co-workers come to know the Lord Jesus Christ, and Tina was one of those individuals. I had the awesome blessing and privilege of seeing her come to Christ during that time and the great honor of seeing her grow in her faith. Her child-like faith had always made me smile in my heart.

Seeing her again when I first arrived on this second deployment was an encouragement to me knowing that she would be working in one of the medical facilities that I would be sending patients to.

Over the last few years since I had served with her, Tina had been through many difficult trials in life and had found that her faith wavered at times. Her daughter Hannah was born three years ago and that time had been both rewarding and challenging for her.

She knew she had not done things the way God wanted her to, and she struggled for many years with returning to church because of a deep feeling of unworthiness. She had a strong sense that God was not pleased with her, and, even more than that, she was not pleased with herself.

During the time that she spent deployed in Iraq, Tina found a renewed sense of strong faith in Christ which blossomed in her life. Some of the things she saw and experienced served to give her the right perspective on life:

"Life must be lived through Christ, don't go through life without him. There are going to be many things that happen in your life that you will need Him to get through, don't keep him out.

"Apart from my normal medical responsibilities for my patients, I feel that my job is to make sure they know that we care and that they are not going to be alone. I try to talk to each of them and get them to think of things other than what is happening."

Tina felt that her role in comforting and showing each one love and compassion was just as important as the medical care they were receiving.

For one patient the medical team was having a very hard time getting a central intravenous line going, and they ended up having to go through his neck. He was really uncomfortable and scared, so Tina took his hand and held it. He began to calm down, and they were able to proceed.

A few minutes later she let go of his hand to do something, and he began to become anxious again. The doctor looked at her and said, "Just keep holding his hand."

So, that's just what she did for the whole procedure Her human touch made an enormous impact for this Marine.

"I feel that God uses the human touch to comfort and reassure people that He is there. This case made me realize that my role, just holding his hand, made a huge difference. I was praying for him the whole time, and I know God was using me."

Tina also shared with me a defining moment for her when she again felt a strong need to draw close to God. One night three patients came in who had been badly wounded in an incident in Ramadi.

One of the patients had died while en route to the SSTP. She was in the OR with one of the other Marines when he began to ask about his friend, the one who had died. She told him she would find out but that he should just focus on getting through his surgery.

Afterwards she was in post op when this patient came out. He again was asking how his friend was. At that moment the chaplain came in to tell him what had happened to his friend. He broke the news to him and then began to pray with him.

"I felt like I shouldn't have been there at that time, experiencing that moment with them. I felt like I was imposing on their moment as they prayed together. I remembered praying and hoping that the friend who died had God in his life and that his family at home did too.

It was at that moment that it all really hit me—I realized that I really didn't have the kind of relationship with God that I should have. Because that moment dramatically touched me, I started reading my Bible again, going back to church and getting serious about Jesus in my life."

I asked her what specifically about that moment had so touched her. "I know God allowed me to witness that scene because it made me realize that I had to know for sure that I was right with God and that if anything ever happened to me my family would have that assurance that I was with God. God used that time to re-ignite my faith and drive me towards Him. I went through a phase after having my daughter Hanna where I felt totally unworthy of going back to church. I wanted to wait until I felt worthy. I now realize that if everyone did that there would not be too many people in church."

Janet Dewees

Thirty-five year old Lieutenant Commander Janet Dewees, a Nurse Anesthetist, has experienced a journey in faith such as she never experienced before in her life. Growing up in the Methodist church she said she never doubted her faith and always just knew God was there.

In her early adult life she walked away from the church but always continued to have a strong belief that God was real and that He was with her. She never doubted until she came to Iraq. She said there were days that she would question how these horrible things could happen if God was there watching over everyone.

"Every day, at the end of the day, I would go to God in prayer and take my questions and feelings of doubt to Him, and I would always finish each day strong again."

I asked Janet what was the first thing she thought of each time the word came in that there were inbound casualties.

"The first thing I always say to myself is, 'Do I have the skills that these people deserve? Please God, use me to help them through this.'"

Lieutenant Commander Dewees felt so often that the scope and severity of the injuries coming into the facility were so far beyond her capabilities as a provider that she realized early on that it was only by the grace of God that she was able to perform at the high and continuously intense level that she did.

"I know that our team would never have been able to do some of the things we did without God's help. It was just too far beyond our grasp so many times—there is no other way to explain this other than God's hand working through us."

One of the most difficult things for Janet has been those individual patients who came in who were conscious and alert. She would find her heart going out to them and invariably saying to each one, "We're here for you; we're going to take good care of you."

As she would look into their eyes she felt as though she connected with them, and they were looking at her as if to say, "Please, don't let me die, please." It was during these moments that she felt the most helpless.

"Of course we take care of every person who comes in with the very best of our abilities, but there are times that it's just out of our control. You want every one of them to get well and be able to go home to their families and friends, but it doesn't always work out that way."

One Marine in particular had come in with a very bad abdominal injury and had bled out a lot before getting to the SSTP. He was conscious and alert when he arrived, and she was able to talk to him and look into his eyes. She comforted him and reassured him that they were going to take great care of him.

The surgery went amazingly well, and she recalled that the whole team was excited because it seemed that the nearly impossible had been done in saving his life.

Later in the week came word that he had died while in Germany. Janet remembered feeling such an incredible sense of helplessness and a sense of loss for him because she had been a part of the team that had seen such an amazing recovery during his first surgery.

In times like this Janet found that it was hard not to question God. "Why do some make it and some not? Why did everything go so well and then in the end he not make it?

"Here was someone that I had looked into his eyes and told him that we were going to take good care of him, and then he died. I really struggled with that. That is one of the hardest things for all of us—you look into their eyes and make them promises and then they never again open their eyes on this earth."

At this point in our interview Janet had tears rolling down her cheeks as the memory still weighed very heavily on her heart.

"Here was a guy who was perfectly fine when he left; we had done everything right—everything in our power—and yet he still died. It just didn't make sense."

During the remainder of the time we spent together she recalled several of these times with great pain and many tears. I could see the heart of a woman who deeply cared for each person, who felt a heavy responsibility for each Marine, Soldier, and Sailor whom she touched.

I could sense the power of the Holy Spirit during this time as He strategically brought memory after memory to her helping to heal her heart. During those precious moments, God helped to draw Janet into a closer realization of just how much His finger prints covered each situation. Her heart was laid wide open, and He performed a kind of spiritual surgery on His beloved child. He had lovingly applied the healing of his Holy hand to her hurting and wounded spirit.

I asked her if it was hard for her to wonder whether or not those who died knew Jesus as their Lord and Savior.

She said that there was a patient who came in who did end up dying, and the whole team was devastated. As they were finishing with him and preparing him for movement to Mortuary Affairs, the doctor found something with his dog tags that had a verse on it.

"You really need to see this," the doctor had said.

She said "I don't know if I want to see it."

He said, "No, you really need to see this."

She went over and read it; it was a tag with a verse on one side and on the other side was a declaration about his personal faith in Jesus Christ. Janet said that she and the doctor both started sobbing uncontrollably with an over-whelming combination of grief at the loss, yet joy that this man knew Jesus.

"With each person who dies, there are always the thoughts that go through your mind about the person's wife, kids, mom, dad, and friends. How will they take it; will they be ok? Will they know that we did the best we could do to save him?"

At the end of the interview I shifted a bit towards talking to her about her personal journey and how her faith has changed since being in this environment.

She said, "It's funny, but I'm 35, and my best friend out here is 23 years old. She is the reason I now am going to church again. She is why I am growing in my relationship with Christ."

I asked if she thought it was funny that God used an Ensign who was 23 years old to get her, a 35 year old Lieutenant Commander, spiritually back on track with God.

"No doubt, it is funny, but I don't know how I would have done it without her. She has been just incredible."

She was speaking of Ensign Gini Hinrichs.

In closing, I asked Janet what she would say to Jesus if He were to come and sit next to her.

"I would want Him to know that I do believe in Him and that I do trust Him and thank Him for everything in my life. I want to thank Him for giving me the strength and guidance that I've needed to be able to take care of all these people because I'm certainly not worthy of taking care of them. And I would thank Him for guiding me through this whole time as I couldn't have made it without Him."

Again I felt the prompting of the Holy Spirit to ask her what else she would want to say. With more tears she managed to say, "…and that I am sorry for not growing closer to You—I have struggled so much in my faith. Are You really for real because I want you to be real so bad."

These were honest answers from a woman who has struggled and questioned but who has an amazing desire to know her Lord more intimately in her life.

She then looked at me as we were finishing up and said, "I want everyone who reads this to know that they are never alone. No matter what, they are never alone. God is always with them."

With that we concluded. I think we both felt as though we had just been in the presence of the Lord for the last 45 minutes. And do you know something? I knew we were!

Kevin Brown

An equally important role in the Casualty Evacuation process is that of the pilots who fly the patients and provide security for the medical helicopter as it goes into the landing zone. I had the opportunity to speak to 1ˢᵗ Lt Kevin Brown, a Marine Corps Super Cobra pilot who often flies security in support of CASEVAC missions.

Kevin was serving with the Marine Light Attack Helicopter (HMLA) Squadron-367 based out of Al Taqaddum, Iraq during my time there. Primarily his job was to fly combat missions in support of convoy operations and to provide direct fire support for ground troops. About 30 to 40% of his missions include flying in direct support of CASEVAC missions.

All missions flown in Iraq carry a certain amount of risk and danger to the pilots. There is always a certain level of adrenaline that surges through each pilot when the mission gets underway. However, there is something more urgent about flying in support of Casualty Evacuations because if the "bell" rings (this is the alarm on the flight line for CASEVAC) something bad has already happened.

Each pilot knows that time is of the essence and the execution of his mission is critical and directly impacts how quickly a patient will ultimately get on to the operating table. Lt Brown said that all pilots are conditioned to react to the ringing of any bell, sometimes finding themselves jumping into action impulsively at any sound resembling the CASEVAC bell.

"We train extensively as Cobra pilots to shave off critical minutes in our launch times so that we don't delay the mission in any way. We try to get the time it takes to put on our vest from 15 seconds to 2 seconds. We train to get the birds armed in 40 seconds not 2 minutes. We do anything we can to be ready because we know we are working within a critical 'Golden Hour' window to give these guys the best possible chance."

Spiritually speaking, I asked Kevin if there was anything special he does when he knows he is going in support of a CASEVAC mission.

"I pray before each mission because I know I need God's strength to do my best."

He shared with me that he had a strong faith prior to coming to Iraq, but his time in the combat zone has served to kind of "hone" his faith. I asked him what that meant.

He said, "Before I came here, I was trying to get everything done before my life went on hold for seven months.

I was trying to get in all the time I could with my friends, girlfriend and family as well as going everywhere and experiencing everything I could. When you are in this mode it is extremely hard to spend quality time with God.

Coming here has given me the ability to have all the distractions of my normal life removed and the opportunity to focus completely on my relationship with Christ. So many times the world gets in the way of our ability to walk as closely with God as we would like to."

Lt Brown's statement was a confirmation for me as I looked back on the foundational principal God has taught me about turning the volume down on life and getting intimate with Him. This fact seems to be surfacing over and over again on the battlefield for those who are believers in Jesus. Every person I've talked to has this in common.

With the distractions of everyday life gone, one's walk with God is intensified dramatically.

The seriousness of the situation in Iraq was really driven home hard for Kevin during one of the first CASEVAC missions he flew. An urgent Nine-Line (this is the form we use to report injuries on the battlefield) came in for a patient from Ramadi. The team worked flawlessly, and they were able to get over to the pickup site very quickly.

Once the CH-46 helicopter was on the ground in the landing zone Lt Brown and his Pilot in Command continued to circle overhead in a defensive pattern around the pick up site. Normally, when the helicopter is on the deck, the patients are immediately loaded into the bird, and they lift off again.

On this occasion it was nearly five minutes, and the patient still had not been loaded on the bird. The Pilot in Command radioed down to the bird on the ground to inquire about the delay.

The bird on the deck said it was going to be a few more minutes, so the Cobra came in and set down next to the CH-46 that was waiting.

Then came word that gave them a strong dose of the sobering reality-the patient had died in the ambulance right before they could load him on the helicopter.

From Kevin's vantage point in the cockpit of the Cobra only 15 or 20 feet away, he could see that instead of loading a patient, the crew loaded a black body bag into the back of the waiting CH-46 helicopter. It was as though all of them watched in slow motion as this fallen comrade was put into the helicopter for his final escort from the battlefield.

It was at that moment that 1st Lt Kevin Brown came to the understanding of the serious nature of the role of the United States in Iraq. People were dying; some people would never go home alive from this battlefield.

"Obviously, for the medical professionals, it's a little bit different because they deal with life and death up close and personal all the time. That is their job as trauma nurses and trauma surgeons. For us, as gunship pilots, usually it is more at a distance. So for us it was a different experience to get an up close view of this guy getting loaded into the CH-46. Was it a defining moment? I don't know, but it was the moment when we all realized that we were playing for keeps."

"When you're flying CASEVAC's you want to believe that if you do your job the right way, which for us basically means being fast and being good, and if the CH-46 pilots are good, which they are, and if the docs are good, which they are, and we get the guy to the facility within that hour, then he should make it. Those are the rules, right?

That's not always the case. Sometimes we do the very best that we can, and they still will not make it."

It was those times when they could not have done anything better or faster yet the patient still died that Kevin felt the most helpless.

"It is during those times when your faith becomes very important."

For Kevin, although his helicopter does not have the patients in the back, he is responsible to get them where they are going safely. "You feel a real sense of ownership and responsibility for that flight. You don't have the wounded in the back, but you are the one responsible for getting them where they need to go."

For all his contributions and efforts while here he said he definitely doesn't feel like a hero or like he did anything that extraordinary.

"I've tried to make a difference in the lives of the people around me, especially those who work for me. I feel like after being here I have a much better perspective on life. It was humbling because I was a part of something that was much, much bigger than I am."

I asked Kevin as we closed what he would most want people back home to know if he had the chance to tell them.

"I would say two things. The first would be that a personal faith in Christ is critical, especially in hard times.

Without that, everything in life is more difficult. The second thing is service. Take some time out of your life to serve other people. Regardless of what capacity you serve, find some way that you can serve others. There is nothing more rewarding than that."

CASEVAC section of CH-46 helicopters on standby

SSTP team unload a wounded Marine

CH-46 dropping off casualty to awaiting ambulance

Famous 1st Marine Division motto
above entrance to palace compound

Exterior of the Camp Blue Diamond chapel

Inside the chapel

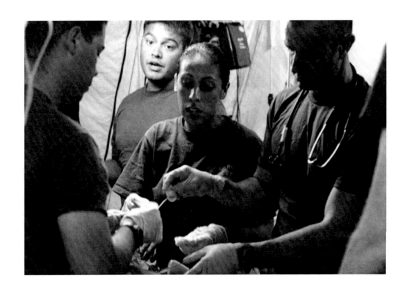

HM3 Tina Terrones lends a hand in the operating room

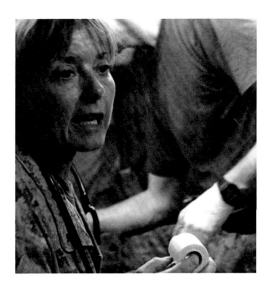

LCDR Susan Pennebecker shows
resolve during continuous medical operations

A Gunny from 3rd LAR holds an Iraqi boy

Female soldier shows great courage before surgery

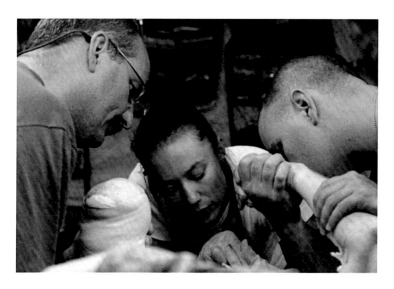

LCDR Janet Dewees and team preparing
to inform a Marine of the loss of his right arm

LCDR Dewees ventilating patient

"Doc" Chambers and his team with
an Iraqi family following treatment

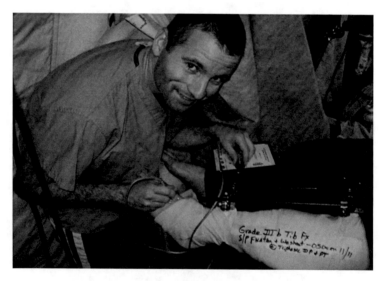

"Doc" Chambers doing a final circulation
check with a patient prior to transport

Rockets and mortars are an everyday part of life in Iraq

ENS Gini Hinrichs holding
an Iraqi boy who lost his family

Chief Suzi Dugger comforts an Iraqi child

Chaplain comforts two grieving
Marines who have just lost a buddy

CAPT Daniel Gade and friends
prior to 10 January 2005

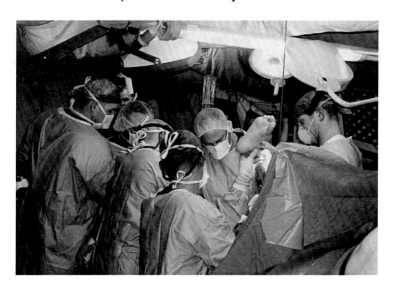

Doctor Chambers and team
work feverishly on Daniel Gade

Daniel Gade six months after being wounded

Daniel and Wendy Gade with President Bush
presenting the captain with two Purple Hearts

Bridge across the Euphrates River in Ramadi

Barbed wire atop the perimeter of Camp Taqaddum

GEN Hagee, Commandant of the
Marine Corps with the SSTP team

ENS Hinrichs with the SGTMAJ of the Marine Corps

1st Lt Kevin Brown in his
AH-1W Super Cobra in Taqaddum

Damage to ambulance caused by suicide bomber

Camp Blue Diamond Chief Petty Officers' Mess

Bible study group

Playing my guitar seconds before
a barrage of rockets impacted the base

Playing guitar with HM1 Hernandez
one day prior to both of our coming home

…in both combat and spiritual warfare

The proverbial picture
that is worth a thousand words

Part 2

Day 1

God Is in Control

"The earth is the Lord's, and all its fullness, the world and those who dwell therein."
—Psalm 24:1

8 September 2004

As the days draw on here there is an element of settling in that has taken place. My sleep schedule seems to be somewhat normalized, and I am on shift from 7 p.m. to 7 a.m. To date we have been somewhat fortunate that not too much has happened to coalition or American troops until yesterday when we had four killed in action (KIA). The authorities and chain of command refer to them as "Fallen Angels."

These times are especially hard for me because the fate of these troops hangs on my quick actions to dispatch and get them to an appropriate medical facility—or does it? God alone holds us in His hands and when our time is up, it is up. No amount of quick decision making on my part will be able to save someone whom God has determined will go. This I struggle with. I still do my very best to move these troops quickly and pray that God will protect and heal each one of them.

Do we hold our own destiny in our hands, or does God reserve that right completely? I believe the only thing we do have control over is the decision to live right for Him now, to ensure that our every breath is for Him in service of His Kingdom.

We don't know when a roadside bomb or a heart attack or a drunk driver will take us or our loved ones. In the words of Jesus in the last Chapter of John, *"If I will that he remain until I return, what is that to you? You follow me."* (John 21:22)

We don't know when our end will come, but we can "follow Him." To some this may seem scary. But to master this in your heart of hearts is to truly live in freedom and with determined purpose. Nothing else under the sun matters but what is done for the Kingdom.

Have you asked yourself today, what have I done for God's purposes rather than my own? Do you roll through life with a sense of self or a sense of salvation? Is there someone God has placed in your path that you could affect for Him? Almost assuredly the answer is yes.

The more we get out of the way and get over ourselves the more God can use us and work through us. I compel you brothers and sisters to run the good race, fight the good fight and storm the gates of hell—not in your own power, but the power of the Almighty. Surrender yourself with reckless abandon, you won't be sorry!

As I sit here I am reminded of the pain in my heart as I am separated from my precious Kellee, my wife who completes me. There is a sense of loss, but with the loss comes an acute sense of purpose in the Spirit. Friends, live your life with purpose, HIS Purpose!

From the Battlefield,
Pastor Ryan
Ramadi, Iraq

Application:

We as humans have this nasty habit called self-reliance and independence. These are good qualities when in the work place, but when it comes to our relationship with Christ, it can be a real spiritual hindrance. Too many of us have the bumper sticker on our spiritual vehicle that says, "God is my co-pilot." Actually, we need to move over and let Him take the wheel! Understanding that God is the one who calls the shots will help us release to Him some of those heavy things we feel responsible for, and trust Him in a greater way.

Prayer:

Lord, so many times we feel like we have to make things happen in our life. We shoulder the responsibility for the ultimate outcome of everything we do. We find Lord that more times than not we resemble Martha rather than Mary. Help us, Lord, to release our burdens to You and rest in the knowledge that You have all things under control in our life. By faith we release these things to You today.

In Jesus' Name, Amen.

Day 2

For Such a Time as This

"And who knows but that you have come to royal positions for such a time as this."
—Esther 4:14

11 September 2004

I am amazed at the events of this past week. My heart has endured trial and pain in the midst of the chaos in this land. How could it be that You God have placed me here? This question is one that I'm sure Esther asked herself when as a Jew she found herself queen of a heathen kingdom and the wife of a heathen king.

"Oh Lord, how is it that I am in this place? I had other plans, other dreams for my life."

I think we all find ourselves asking these same questions when things don't go as we thought they would or should.

"But Lord, I have a church to run. But Lord, I have a wife getting ready to graduate from college and a son in his last year of high school. Why do I have to go?"

Esther found herself in the King's palace with a position of honor, privilege and influence. In fact verse 2:15 says, *"She won the favor of all who saw her."* The scripture goes on to say,

"For if you remain silent at this time, relief and deliverance for the Jews will arise from another place, but you and your father's family will perish. And who knows but that you have come to royal positions for such a time as this."

—Esther 4:14

We do not always know right away why we are in the position or place we are, but we can be assured that it is for God's purpose so that His light can shine during times of darkness.

I have asked myself this same question these past few weeks. All at once it hit me. I am in the command center with my finger on the pulse of everything that happens in this country. I know of bombing missions, raids and actions before they occur. I know of every person who is wounded or killed when it happens. I sit behind the Commanding General who comes to me directly for news of his Marines and Sailors.

Could it be that I have been placed in this position of privilege for such a time as this? *Yes!* To be able to pray while things are happening; to be able to activate the prayer chains immediately when someone is wounded; to intercede for this nation and its people.

This week already has seen much loss of life and many wounded. Five times I have had to give news or confirm deaths of best friends, family members and co-workers to those around me. The news is overwhelming to those who have to hear about their friend or loved one.

The look on their faces I will not soon forget. It is at this time that I pray for them—even before I tell them— that I might be in a position to bring comfort and relief in the midst of pain and to encourage them with the power of the Gospel and God's never-ending love for us.

Could it be that I am here for such a time as this—in the nerve center of this war? Again, *yes!*

All of us find ourselves in these places in life. Places we don't want to be, doing things we don't want to do around people we don't want to be around. Know this, you are there for God's purpose. Make God Lord over every situation and pray a prayer that I have always prayed:

"Lord, send me at least one person that I can minister to or be a blessing to today."

You will be surprised at how He answers this prayer. Never let an opportunity that He has placed before you pass by. Do not despise your circumstances; arise in the power of the Holy Spirit.

Blessings from Babylon,
Pastor Ryan
Ramadi, Iraq

Application:

Have you found yourself in a place lately that caused you to wonder what possible good could come from this? Perhaps it's a new job or a new class, or maybe it's a new boss or trouble in a marriage. Stop and consider what purpose God could have for you to be where you are and who He may want you to influence for His Kingdom. It could be that despite an uncomfortable situation God wants to work through you to touch someone with His love or to influence the outcome of an otherwise hopeless situation. Consider this; then change your outlook to His outlook!

Prayer:

Lord, when I find myself in a place that I don't really like, enjoy, or see a purpose in, help me to look at the situation with Your eyes and Your perspective. Help me, Lord, to be content with where I am and take on the heart of Joseph who said: "Those things that you meant for evil, God has meant them for good." Give me a pure heart to seek you and find your purpose in every place. Please lead me to at least one person today that I can share Your love with.

In Your Name, Amen.

Day 3

Count It All Joy

"Count it all joy when we fall into various trials…"
—James 1:2

17 September 2004

Can there be any doubt that we serve a mighty God—a God whose power and love is infinite. This week in the war zone there has been good and bad. We have made progress but suffered loss. James says that we are to:

"Count it all joy when we fall into various trials, knowing that the testing of our faith produces patience. But let patience run its course, that you may be perfect and complete, lacking nothing."
—James 1:2-3

I look at this verse and I look at my environment and say to myself, "God must really want me to be perfect and complete lacking nothing because there are certainly 'various trials.' I'm still having difficulty with 'count it all joy.' With God's help I will some day be able to perfect this part."

It's never easy to walk in love and display joy when the world is literally blowing up around you. Losing Marines, Sailors, and Soldiers is not my idea of fun, and it's hard to have joy in this. God's Word declares that we are to put on His joy during these times—not joy at what is happening, but joy *in spite* of what is happening.

To master this is truly a work of God in our life. To declare as Job did, "though He slay me, yet will I serve Him..." Looking at all of these things I remind myself that in the midst of death, suffering and hardship it is still possible to put on the joy of the Lord.

The toll this week for us has been high. The toll in the world this week has been high. For we have had terrorist bombings, children murdered, hurricanes and typhoons, and political tension...and yet we are to count it all joy.

Count it all joy when we are persecuted and hated for His name. Count it all joy when our children are sick. Count it all joy when we lose our job. Count it all joy when we find ourselves alone and separated from the ones we love. Count it all joy? Yes!

If I see another kid blown up or shot I'll break down...Count it all joy. If I see another child wounded by a roadside bomb, I'll fall apart... Count it all joy. If I miss my wife any more than I already do, I'll throw in the towel... Count it all joy.

Joy comes from knowing the Maker of all things, the One Who died and gave Himself for me. My world might fall apart around me, but He still sits on the throne of my life. This will never change.

If we focus on the storm, surely we will sink into the abyss. If we focus on Jesus, the storm will give way to calm.

Your prayers this week for those wounded have availed much. One young man shot in the face underwent surgery and was able to be repaired with minimal long-term affects. Of course, there will be a scar, but he will be able to function normally again. Can there be any doubt that we serve a mighty God? Until next week, stay focused on Jesus and count it all joy!

In Christ,
Pastor Ryan
Ramadi, Iraq

Application:

Have the storms of your life come to an all time high? The scriptures declare to us that Joy is not dependent upon our environment or circumstances. When we look at our situation through God's lens our perspective will soon come into the proper focus. Take the truth of God's Word, and apply it liberally to your heart, allowing the Holy Spirit to surround you and restore the joy of your salvation.

Prayer:

Lord, I often find that I view the reality of my life through my circumstances. I know that this is not what You have called me to do. Please strengthen my heart and attitude that it would come into line with the truth of Who You are and the truth of Your Word. Help me Lord to put on Your joy no matter where I find myself in life. I want to have the heart of Paul and Silas who sang praise songs while chained in prison. Grant me this reality in my life Lord, and please lead me to at least one person today that I can share Your love with.

In Your Name, Amen.

Day 4

Don't Lose Heart

"In the world you will have tribulation; but be of good cheer, I have overcome the world.
— John 16:33

25 September 2004

This week as I write I pause to think of all the chaos our world has seen over the last few weeks. Sometimes the things going on here in this troubled part of the world pale in comparison to other places—the crisis in the Sudan, the suffering in Haiti with scores dead and 1200 still missing, the southern part of the United States ravaged by hurricanes and the Far East with its typhoons, the horrible scene in Russia regarding children and families… .

It would be easy for us to lose heart in times like these, but a close examination of the scripture gives us hope.

Jesus declares in Matthew 24 when asked by His disciples when will the end be?

"Take heed that no one deceives you. For many will come in My name, saying, 'I am the Christ,' and will deceive many. And you will hear of wars and rumors of wars. See that you are not troubled; for all these things must come to pass, but the end is not yet. For nation will rise against nation, and kingdom against kingdom. And there will be famines, pestilences, and

earthquakes in various places. All these are the be-
ginning of sorrows. "Then they will deliver you up to
tribulation and kill you, and you will be hated by all
nations for My name's sake. And then many will be of-
fended, will betray one another, and will hate one an-
other. Then many false prophets will rise up and de-
ceive many. And because lawlessness will abound, the
love of many will grow cold. But he who endures to
the end shall be saved. And this gospel of the kingdom
will be preached in all the world as a witness to all
the nations, and then the end will come.

—Matthew 24:4-14

At first glance this passage would seem to indicate a news report from CNN. Sometimes looking around us it is easy to do one of two things—either run for the hills because the Lord is about to come and nothing else matters in life, or begin to try to predict when the Lord will return.

The scriptures also declare that we will not know the day or the hour, but we will know the season. We are in the season! I believe the lesson in this is to maintain balance. We must not have our bags packed at the door just yet. We must allow the Holy Spirit to make us ready—spiritually— for the great Soul Harvest that accompanies this season we are in.

We must resist the temptation to have tunnel vision as we are "looking up because our redemption draws near." We must not forget that around us are thousands who are lost and in need of the Savior. The events of this week can truly give us a broken heart, but God uses broken hearts to impact His Kingdom.

"The Lord is not slack concerning His promise, as
some count slackness, but is long suffering toward us,

not willing that any should perish but that all should come to repentance."

—2 Peter 3:9

Run the race friends. Take up your cross and pursue the upward calling of the Lord Jesus Christ. Yes, the time is near, but it is not here yet. There is much work to be done.

Again, I remind you of a simple prayer that I pray each day, "Lord, lead me to at least one person today that I can share Your love with." Until next week, I pray God's hand of mercy is upon you and upon this battlefield.

In His loving arms,
Pastor Ryan
Ramadi, Iraq

Application:

Many times in our zeal for the Lord we can find that we become ineffective in our witness for Him. Sometimes we get too zealous because of our belief that the end could come at anytime, and without meaning to, we turn people off to the Gospel. Other times, we can find that we do the opposite and stop preparing for the future. God's Word teaches us that we must be balanced. We must be ready at anytime, but carry on from day to day as though the Day of His coming is still far off. Make the most of each day as you labor for the Kingdom.

Prayer:

Holy Father, I come before You today with a heart to serve You, desiring a greater measure of wisdom in my life to witness for You. Help me to understand the gravity of Your return that is so near while balancing my daily life and walk with You to be as effective as possible in my witness. Please lead me to at least one person today that I can share Your love with.

In Your Name, Amen.

Day 5

Unwavering Faith

"Do not lay your hand on the lad, or do anything to him; for now I know that you fear God, since you have not withheld your son, your only son, from Me."

—Genesis 22:12

2 October 2004

This week has been a good week overall on the battlefield in our area. Good is a relative term, which does not necessarily mean good to all, but good in that very few casualties have occurred this week. Very few have lost their lives.

Good you say? Good when you look at the week before and the week before that. Good in that the faithful prayers of all of you have delivered so many from harm. Good in that six children who could have easily died all survived by the grace of our Lord.

It is no coincidence that I have been doing a careful study through the book of Job. Job is a book that not many of us fully understand, including yours truly. Why would a loving God who obviously favored Job allow the Prince of Darkness the opportunity to reap havoc on his life and family? I think a careful study of the Word of God reveals much. In the RSV translation it says this:

"No temptation has overtaken you that is not common to man. God is faithful, and he will not let you be tempted beyond your strength, but with the temptation will also provide the way of escape, that you may be able to endure it."

—1 Corinthians 10:13

So, you might be tempted to say God caused Job's horrible situation, when in fact, the culprit was Lucifer himself. You might say, but God allowed this to happen by giving Satan the freedom to do so. There are several ways you can look at this.

First, by looking at the above verse we realize that God knew first and foremost how much His servant Job could handle and still glorify His name. For we see the response of Job in chapter two following the loss of all his family, his possessions and finally his health:

"Then his wife said to him, "Do you still hold fast your integrity? Curse God, and die." But he said to her, "You speak as one of the foolish women would speak. Shall we receive good at the hand of God, and shall we not receive evil?" In all this Job did not sin with his lips."

—Job 2:9-10

Second, we see that Satan is not able to do or cause anything to God's people unless God allows it. Satan can jeer us, poke at us, tempt us, but he can't lay a hand on us or those things that God has given us unless God allows it.

Third, we find that this case is not the norm in the scriptures. This thing which happened to Job happened to one who could endure the tribulation without compromise. A similar type of test occurred with Abraham and his son Isaac:

> *"And Abraham stretched out his hand and took the knife to slay his son. But the Angel of the Lord called to him from heaven and said, "Abraham, Abraham!" So he said, "Here I am." And He said, "Do not lay your hand on the lad, or do anything to him; for now I know that you fear God, since you have not withheld your son, your only son, from Me."*
>
> —Genesis 22:9-11

We find that Abraham did not waver in his obedience to God. Job, likewise, did not waver in his commitment to God and did not charge God with evil. During his pain, he longed for death to ease his suffering, but he never sinned against God. It is clear to me that the lesson found in Job is not a lesson of "see, God does allow bad things to happen," but rather, "God knows our hearts."

Job's suffering gives us an object lesson on the nature of God and the limited power of Satan. It also shows us that God alone knows how much we can endure and will never give us more than we can handle. It just so happens that spiritual giants like Job and Abraham can handle a whole lot more than most.

It is clear that all the apostles suffered for the Lord Jesus and, in fact, Paul considered that he had been counted worthy to suffer. As we grow in Christ and mature in our commitment to Him, it is likely that there will be times that we will suffer for the sake of the Gospel, not because God delights in our pain, but rather because we, His servants, should delight in Him no matter the cost!

Paul says in his second letter to Timothy:

> *"So do not be ashamed to testify about our Lord, or ashamed of me His prisoner. But join with me in suffering for the Gospel, by the power of God, Who has saved us and called us to holy life-not because of any-*

thing we have done but because of His own purpose and grace."

—2 Tim 1:8-9

My friends, my hope is that none of us would experience loss or pain in life. However, according to the Scripture this is unrealistic. So then my prayer becomes, "Oh Lord, strengthen us to bear up Your Holy Name in times of trouble and trial. May we always glorify You with our actions and words in spite of our circumstances. I pray Lord that You would shape us and mold us into a vessel of honor, ready for every good work for the sake of Your Kingdom."

It would be easy for many of us on the battlefield to question God and ask why He allows such horrible things to happen. We are faced with those things daily, but may we always have a Kingdom perspective in suffering rather than a suffering perspective in the Kingdom.

Grant us Lord the strength to say as Paul did, *"I have fought the good fight, I have finished the race, I have kept the faith."* (2 Timothy 4:7)

May the Lord bless you and keep you in His perfect will always, this day and everyday.

Pastor Ryan
Ramadi, Iraq

Application:

Many times in life we will be faced with those who ask, "How can a loving God allow such horrible things to happen?" We may ourselves even ask this same question at times. We must in our daily life learn to view circumstances through the lens of the scripture and a "God's eye" view rather than our earthly and limited perspective. Apply the truth of God's Word and nature to every circumstance and you will find that His peace will find you even if we don't always have the answers to life's hardest questions.

Prayer:

Lord of all creation, Father of heaven and earth, today we acknowledge that Your ways are higher than ours, Your knowledge greater than ours. Help us Lord in all things to realize who You are and in that knowledge trust You in all things. Help us when we don't understand to take our fears and questions to You by faith knowing that in You all things exist and are sustained. We know we will not always understand Your ways, but we do know You. And because we know You and Your nature and character, we trust that in all things Your perfect will is accomplished.

In Your Holy Name, Amen.

Day 6

The Fear of the Lord

"The fear of the Lord is the beginning of wisdom, And the knowledge of the Holy One is understanding."

—Proverbs 9:10

5 October 2004

Today I have been meditating on a situation I had the occasion to observe last night in the chow hall during evening dinner. Halfway through my meal as several hundred Marines, Soldiers, Sailors, and civilians ate their dinner, I noticed the General came in to eat.

As he waited in line to get his food, nearly everyone was somewhat conscious of his presence with us—some going out of their way to acknowledge a "Good evening sir!" while some were going out of their way to avoid him. If you ever pictured in your mind what a typical general looks like, you would picture this man—confident, strong, intelligent—one who commands respect simply by his presence.

As I watched the General find his way through the line and get his drink, he scanned the many tables for a place to sit. Those having empty spots at their tables seemed to be nervous thinking that perhaps the General would sit down next to or across from them. I watched as he found a table with several other officers. There was one chair open; he found his spot and sat down.

139

The part that I found most interesting about this event is that the person on the other side of where he sat down was a young Lance Corporal who immediately had a look of fear and discomfort on his face as soon as he realized that the General had just sat down across from him. He didn't know whether to stand, sit, or go elsewhere.

The General tried to put him at ease and insisted that he stay where he was. I found this moment in time comical, and yet, I felt for this young guy. It was obvious that he did *not* enjoy his meal and was very uncomfortable.

The Holy Spirit began to speak to my heart about this scene. The lesson was one of God speaking to me about having a healthy fear of Him. Did I have it? This Lance Corporal had a very healthy fear of the General; it was clearly all over his face.

The General is actually a very personable and nice man as on several occasions I have been with him during briefs and in various dealings within the Command Operations Center. He is a pleasant, even compassionate man, but this Lance Corporal did not know this.

The General is concerned and cares about each person under his command and does all in his power to ensure they are safe and taken care of. In fact, there is not much this man would not do for his troops.

Do I have a healthy fear of my God? If there is anything in my life that is not right or any sin big or small, do I fear my God? I understand that God loves me and wants the very best for me in all things, but do I fear Him—not a shaking in my skin type of fear, but a true reverence and Holy respect for Who He is as Lord and God.

A few years ago there was a t-shirt circulating that had a picture of Jesus on the front of it that said "Jesus is my homeboy." While I am not opposed to thinking of Our Lord as a friend who sticks closer than a brother, I do have a hard time diminishing His place to a casual "homeboy" position. This seems to truly lack reverence or respect. To add to my suspicion, those who were wearing this T-shirt were folks who were anything but followers of Christ including several rock stars, actors, and adult models.

The Hebrew word used for fear in this example is the word *yir'ah* which means "awesome or terrifying thing (object causing fear), fear (of God), respect, reverence, piety, or revered."

The presence of the General caused all of these emotions and caused all who were around to check themselves. They automatically wondered if their shirt was untucked, or uniform worn properly, or do I have a good haircut? Are we always conscious of the "GENERAL" who is ever with us?

This knowledge of the Holy One and realization that He is at our table, in our car, in our home, at our place of work could just give us the incentive we need to stop the next time we think about sinning. The scripture says:

> *"The fear of the Lord is the beginning of wisdom, And the knowledge of the Holy One is understanding."*
>
> —Proverbs 9:10

Try to remember my friends that the GENERAL is with us always. He knows each of us by name and has our very best interests and welfare in mind.

God bless you all!
Pastor Ryan
Ramadi, Iraq

Application:

The world is full of people, even Christians who have a view of God as a God of love. This is great except when the other part is left out. What other part? The part about His also being the righteous and Holy Judge. If we only think of God as a harp playing, soft spoken, loving friend, (or perhaps our homeboy) we lose our healthy fear and reverence for Him. Part of serving Christ effectively is also revering and respecting Him as Lord over all. The love part is easy; it's the other part that we find more difficult. Begin to cultivate a healthy fear of God in your life, and I promise, your relationship with Him will only get better.

Prayer:

Lord, we find that it is very easy to consider how much You love us. You love us so much you sent Jesus to the Cross in our place. Sometimes Lord we forget that You are also a Righteous Judge. Lord, may we gain a greater reverence and a healthy fear of You as well. Help us to balance these two things as we walk with You day by day. Thank You that You are a God of love, and that You are Holy and Just.

In Jesus' Name, Amen.

Day 7

Courage Under Fire

"Be strong and of good courage, do not fear nor be afraid of them; for the LORD your God, He is the One who goes with you. He will not leave you nor forsake you."

—Deuteronomy 31:6

9 October 2004

"…On a separate occasion, he was providing medical coverage for his platoon when they immediately began taking heavy enemy direct machine gun fire, accurate sniper fire, RPG (Rocket Propelled Grenade) and indirect mortar fire. During the 90-minute fierce firefight a Marine was shot in the head, requiring urgent medical treatment. He immediately, and with disregard for his own safety, rushed from his position through the deadly machine gun and sniper fire to the position where the Marine lay wounded. Upon arriving at the scene he noticed that the Marines manning the position were stunned by the condition of the casualty, had slowed their rate of fire on the enemy, and were being pinned down by the heavy enemy fire. He quickly assessed the situation, took charge, issued orders to the stunned Marines to increase their rate of fire, and began providing first aid to the wounded Marine. While conducting first aid, the wounded Marine went into shock, and needed to be medically evacuated. He calmly took charge of the situation, developed a course of action to move the injured Marine, and safely moved the wounded Marine while directing the Marines' fire. His actions motivated the Marines in the surrounding positions to provide over-whelming suppressive fire while the casualty was carried across heavy direct and indirect fire to the waiting ambu-lance. He remained with the casualty during the mobile medical evacuation and continued treating him. He success-fully controlled the bleeding and stabilized the Marine, sav-ing his life…"

*   *   *

To many this may sound like a Medal of Honor cita-tion for a hospital corpsman or medic from Vietnam or WWII—or to some, maybe a script for the latest Tom Clancy war thriller or a new Mel Gibson movie. To me it is the account of an actual event occurring several weeks ago here in Iraq. I have documentation of not just this one, but many others very similar to it.

I am reminded of the words of Admiral Chester Nimitz concerning the Marines' battle for Iwo Jima from 19 February to 16 March 1945: "Uncommon valor is a common virtue."

This type of heroism is happening every day in Iraq. Consistently, Marines, Sailors, and Soldiers place them-selves at great risk to rescue a comrade or to ensure the safety of their platoon. Why am I sharing this with you?

First, because just reading this account sends chills down my spine and causes me to stick my chest out with pride. The knowledge of the type of people I serve with every day can't help but make one proud of the rich heri-tage of the brave men and women who have gone before us as well as those who are here now.

Secondly, because it draws a strong real-life symbol of the spiritual battle that we are engaged in as believers every day. We as Christians are under a constant barrage of enemy fire in every part of life. The calculated attack of the enemy and his cohorts can be seen reaping havoc on brothers and sisters every day.

There are, however, scores of faithful Saints who brave the fiery arrows of the wicked one and rush to the aid of those who are emotionally and spiritually wounded in action. At great personal risk to self, drawing the fire of the enemy, they brave the attack and minister the grace and love of Jesus Christ to those most in need.

The Apostle Paul's résumé looks like this:

"...in labors more abundant, in stripes above measure, in prisons more frequently, in deaths often. From the Jews five times I received forty stripes minus one. Three times I was beaten with rods; once I was stoned; three times I was shipwrecked; a night and a day I have been in the deep; in journeys often, in perils of waters, in perils of robbers, in perils of my own countrymen, in perils of the Gentiles, in perils in the city, in perils in the wilderness, in perils in the sea, in perils among false brethren; in weariness and toil, in sleeplessness often, in hunger and thirst, in fastings often, in cold and nakedness, besides the other things, what comes upon me daily: my deep concern for all the churches."

—2 Corinthians 11:23-28

During the onslaught of perils that Paul faced, his concern was not for himself, but rather the zealous furtherance of the Gospel and the well being of the church. The enemy attacks with the ferociousness of a lion, but even the lion falls by the sword (the Word of God). Take up your armor, mighty warriors of Christ, and rush into the face of enemy fire. Do not worry about yourself,

God has your back!

"For though we walk in the flesh, we do not war according to the flesh. For the weapons of our warfare are not carnal but mighty in God for pulling down strongholds, casting down arguments and every high thing that exalts itself against the knowledge of God..."

—2 Corinthians 10:3-5a

I urge you brethren by the mercies of God that you present yourselves, as a living sacrifice...for this is your reasonable service. Run the race and fight the fight. Be filled with the Mighty Holy Spirit and make a difference in this world for the Kingdom of God.

Until next week brothers and sisters, God bless you and keep you in His mighty Way.

Pastor Ryan
Ramadi, Iraq

Application:

So many times in life we find that fear holds us back from going forward with God's purpose, or what we may think is God's purpose for our life. When we allow fear to hold us back we are really displaying a lack of trust in God's plan. If He is guiding us forward or leading us, we need not fear what man can do to us or what man can say about us. When we trust completely in the Object of our faith it gives us courage to forge ahead no matter what our circumstances say. Trust His voice and take His hand; He will never lead you astray!

Prayer:

Lord, when I fear, when I falter, please strengthen me by Your Holy Spirit to get up and take another step. Strengthen me to reach higher and go further than before. Remove my fear and my doubt and restore my confidence in You and You alone. Lift me up in my weakness and show Yourself to be strong in me. For it is You and You alone who I trust and rely upon. I give You my everything this day and stand ready to forge ahead in boldness knowing that You are right by my side.

In Jesus' Name, Amen.

Day 8

The Voice of the Lord

"My sheep hear My voice, and I know them, and they follow Me."

—John 10:27

16 October 2004

For the better part of two weeks now, God has been speaking to me about hearing His voice and using examples from my current environment to drive home the lesson. I have been here for nearly two months now and would no longer consider my self a Camp Blue Diamond rookie, but more of a veteran of the battlefield.

You might say; how does one become a veteran in less than two months? The answer is really more a matter of survival and necessity than choice.

The first thing I noticed was that this time around was much different from last year's ground war. The surroundings, the mission, the enemy were all different.

Within 12 hours of arriving I got my first sobering dose of, "You are indeed a rookie." This became very clear to me when the first burst of automatic machine gun fire went off close to me.

I did what any strong, red-blooded American alpha male would do, I ducked so hard I nearly fell over, and I immediately dashed behind the nearest large, heavy object! When I stopped shaking I looked out from my safe place and noticed that everyone was still walking around like nothing had happened.

Of course, I dusted myself off quickly, acting as though nothing had happened and continued about my business. I couldn't help but wonder why in the world no one else took the drastic measures I had. Were they really that much braver than I? Was I a hopeless chicken afraid the sky was falling?

This same exercise continued daily until someone saw me taking drastic self-preservation measures, and gently educated me that the burst of machine gun fire was from the firing range just on the other side of the wall. Boy, did I feel like a dunce. No wonder everyone was walking around like nothing was happening.

In like manner, I also had to be educated on the difference between incoming mortars and outgoing artillery. Again, for the first few weeks whenever there was incoming, everyone would disappear making the streets and camp look like a ghost town. Yeah, I had heard whistles and strange sounds overhead but what was that about?

Well, as it turns out, the little whistles were incoming rockets and mortars and the reason I was walking around on the streets by myself was because everyone else was in the bunkers taking cover. Wow, don't I feel like quite the savvy combat veteran!

To make this situation worse, several minutes later there were several loud booms in a row which sent me running for cover just as everyone else was coming out of the bunkers. Let me guess, not incoming? "Nope," some young Marine corrected me, "that was outgoing artillery."

I was later educated by a grungy senior chief who said, "The difference is where you feel it. If you feel it in your feet up into your legs, it's incoming, impacting. If you feel it in the air from your head down to your waist, it's outgoing."

God began to speak to me through these experiences about coming to know and understand His voice and to distinguish His voice from others.

Jesus said in John 10:

> *"Most assuredly, I say to you, he who does not enter the sheepfold by the door, but climbs up some other way, the same is a thief and a robber. But he who enters by the door is the shepherd of the sheep. To him the doorkeeper opens, and the sheep hear his voice; and he calls his own sheep by name and leads them out. And when he brings out his own sheep, he goes before them; and the sheep follow him, for they know his voice. Yet they will by no means follow a stranger, but will flee from him, for they do not know the voice of strangers." "...My sheep hear My voice, and I know them, and they follow Me."*
>
> —John 10:1-5, 27

I began to think about this. The longer I am here, the more I have become able to distinguish between what is friendly and what is not—those things which are dangerous to me and those that repel the attacks of the enemy.

In the same way, we become more and more able to distinguish the voice of God in our lives as we spend time with Him and in His Word. The better we come to know Him, the more clearly we will hear His voice. God will never lead us contrary to His Word. The more that we come to know His Word the more we will be able to determine if what we are hearing is something God would say, something from our own imagination, or something the enemy is lobbing our way to sidetrack or derail us.

I have been told that there is a certain type of penguin in the arctic who out of a crowded beach of thousands and thousands of baby penguins can immediately pick out the crying of her own chick. That is simply amazing to me.

In the sea of voices and influences trying to lead us and influence us, there is one voice, the voice of Truth that will never lead us astray.

Become more and more acquainted with the Lord Jesus and His Word; spend intimate time with Him in prayer, and before you know it, you will be able to distinguish His voice from the crowd noise without exception. May the Lord bless you and keep you this week.

Pastor Ryan
Ramadi, Iraq

Application:

There are so many things in this world competing for our attention. Someone once said, "The devil doesn't have to get you to sin, he just has to keep you busy." Why is this true? Because he knows if he can keep you occupied with the business of life, you will take your eye off Christ. The hum-drum of daily life will soon drown out the still small voice of the Lord. What's the solution? Turn the volume down on life and get intimate with God. Spend quiet time each day with Him and glean the gold nuggets of knowledge and wisdom that can only come from the living Word.

Prayer:

Lord, sometimes I feel like all I can hear is the confusing sound of life around me. Voices everywhere telling me what I should wear, what I should eat, what I should look like and more. Lord, more than anything else I want to hear Your voice and be found in Your presence each day. Help me to hear Your voice of truth in every circumstance and discipline my life. Please pour Your Spirit into my life fresh and new this day.

In Jesus' Holy Name I pray, Amen.

Day 9

The Danger of Sin

"But your iniquities have made a separation between you and your God, And your sins have hidden His face from you so that He does not hear."

22 October 2004

I have so many examples that God has given me over the past few weeks that I wondered which was for today. As I prayed God began to lead me in the direction of a vivid illustration that could come from no other place than this part of the world. Wednesday night, several hours before I got off shift at midnight, a bad sand storm blew over the whole area and stayed for most of the night; it returned for a while the next morning. Now, I don't know about you, but when I think of a sand storm, I think of blowing sand and debris. I was quite surprised by the characteristics of this one, however. Instead of blowing like crazy and beating everything up, it just settled in. There was no wind, no clouds, nothing. It just appeared over the whole area and sat there.

As I left at midnight to walk the half-mile or so to my room, I had to carefully navigate with my flashlight because I could see no more than 20 feet in front of me and sometimes less. It took me much longer than the normal 10 minutes to get to my destination.

My breathing and my eyes were affected by the fine soot and dust in the air. Prior to leaving the Command Center, the fine dust had infiltrated the building and settled inside, getting into everything. All flights were cancelled that night, not one chopper could fly. All communications equipment was down and not functioning. All convoys and troop movement came to a halt, and weapons systems were nearly non-functional.

We were getting sporadic and broken messages from some of the convoys that they could not go anywhere. The few that tried ended up lost. As I thought about this after getting off work and trekking home, the Lord gave me some striking pictures and parallels for our spiritual life.

The sand storm was a vivid illustration of sin in the life of believers.

First: Sin, like this sand storm, diminishes visibility and damages our ability to see the reality of what God has for us. We become blind to our condition and many times blind to the hidden dangers around us. Even with my flashlight, I remember stumbling several times because of a hole or a rock that I couldn't make out in the sand. Even with my flashlight on, my eyes were affected by the constant presence of particles in the air.

Likewise, spiritually, we stumble through life in a blinded state when we allow sin to settle in on us, not heeding the warnings of the Holy Spirit.

> *"But if your eye is bad, your whole body will be full of darkness. If then the light that is in you is darkness, how great is the darkness!"*
>
> —Matthew 6:23

> *Your glorying is not good. Do you not know that a little leaven leavens the whole lump? Therefore purge out the old leaven, that you may be a new lump..."*
>
> —1 Corinthians 5:6-7

Second: Sin interferes with our communication. Our prayers are hindered to our Heavenly Father when we are laden down with sinful practices, deeds and thoughts. Also, our communication with family, friends, and other believers is hindered. It causes our responses and interaction with others to be less sensitive and more judgmental rather than patient and kind.

"But your iniquities have made a separation between you and your God, And your sins have hidden His face from you so that He does not hear.
—Isaiah 59:2

"We know that God does not hear sinners; but if anyone is God-fearing and does His will, He hears him."
—John 9:31

"If I regard wickedness in my heart, The Lord will not hear."
—Psalm 66:18

"And why do you look at the speck in your brother's eye, but do not perceive the plank in your own eye? Or how can you say to your brother, 'Brother, let me remove the speck that is in your eye,' when you yourself do not see the plank that is in your own eye? Hypocrite! First remove the plank from your own eye, and then you will see clearly to remove the speck that is in your brother's eye."
—Luke 6:41-42

Third: Sin immobilizes us. Those who are laden down in sin are incapable of moving forward with God's purposes and His will for their lives. It affects our ability to see, pray and walk uprightly before God. It clogs our wheels so to speak and renders us "broken down" spiritually.

> *"For those who live according to the flesh set their minds on the things of the flesh, but those who live according to the Spirit, the things of the Spirit. For to be carnally minded is death, but to be spiritually minded is life and peace. Because the carnal mind is enmity against God; for it is not subject to the law of God, nor indeed can be. So then, those who are in the flesh cannot please God."*
>
> —Romans 8:5-8

What is the solution? The solution is to confess our sin to God and get back on track. Don't let the guilt of where you are now prevent you from going to where God wants to take you. The scripture promises:

> *"If we confess our sins, He is faithful and just to forgive us our sins and to cleanse us from all unrighteousness."*
>
> —1 John 1:9

What a wonderful thing for all of us the next morning to have the smothering, choking dust gone and to be able to move about and breathe normally again. In fact, after the experience of the hindrances of the dust, the air the next morning almost seemed better than it had been the previous day! The birds seemed to sing more beautifully, and the sun shone brighter.

Likewise, the person who comes out of the horrible clutches of sin into His marvelous light experiences the beauty and peace that only a right standing with Christ can bring.

Don't get me wrong, the next morning there was a thin layer of dust on *everything*, but through the diligent efforts of all of us in the camp, we were soon able to clean up the mess left behind by the storm.

The same is true for us, when we come out of sin, there will be left over reminders of our going astray, but the good news is that with a little time, God makes all things new. He sanctifies us and cleans us up. Before long, we become an example of what the Apostle Paul was talking about:

> *"Therefore, if anyone is in Christ, he is a new creation; old things have passed away; behold, all things have become new."*
>
> —2 Corinthians 5:17

God bless you and keep you in His perfect will this week—until next week…

Pastor Ryan
Ramadi, Iraq

Application:

Most of us have found ourselves crippled at one point or another by sin, whether intentionally or unintentionally. We sometimes turn around and find ourselves immobilized in our spiritual life and are not sure how we got there or how to get back to where we should be. The answer to this is surprisingly simple, and yet so many find it one of the most difficult steps to take. Rather than confess our sins to God and accept His healing and forgiveness, we place ourselves in spiritual "hyperspace" somewhere between sin and forgiveness. This ought not to be. Apply the truth of God's Holy Word to your situation today and walk in the assurance of His complete forgiveness.

Prayer:

Precious Lord, so many times we find ourselves in a place so hurtful and uncomfortable because we have allowed sin to creep into our lives. It causes us to be far from You and to not hear Your voice. Please give us the strength to turn to You in faith knowing that if we confess our sin to You that You will be faithful to forgive us and wash us clean. Help us to embrace this truth in our lives and to turn away from sinful things, permanently. We know that only through the power of Your loving Holy Spirit can we accomplish this. We submit ourselves to You today in faith,

In Jesus' matchless Name I pray, Amen.

Day 10

The Safety of God's Boundaries

"All things are lawful, but not all things are profitable."

—1 Corinthians 10:23, NASB

29 October 2004

God has given me a myriad of object lessons to choose from, but today, I want to share with you my observations from the battlefield about safe boundaries.

All around me there are limits—limits as to what time you can be out at night without a "Battle Buddy." Basically it is the buddy system for the battlefield. Due to safety concerns, there are limits to where one can go within the city of Ramadi. There are limits as to how much we are able to see outside of the camp due to the 12-foot high, 2-foot thick wall which surrounds the perimeter.

Now it is human nature to want to see what's going on outside and even to want to go and experience the culture of the people—to see how they live and interact with one another, how they interact with us, and to help someone in need. While these seem harmless enough and even admirable intentions, there is far more at stake when going outside these walls.

While walking around the base, I am aware of several things. My surroundings are familiar and even comforting. I am in my element. I am also conscious of the fact that I am, for the most part, safe. I have guard towers every couple hundred feet; I have several thousand Marines and Soldiers around me as well as heavily fortified gates.

Aside from the several times a week that a mortar or rocket hits close to the base or on it, I am relatively safe in our fortress. I, of course, have the added protection of my God which is truly why I am safe.

This brought to mind the striking comparison with how we as Christians many times are prone to get off track when we feel that our faith is too constraining. We feel we are strong and can handle the walk on the outside of the fence. You hear it all the time in conversations.

- "You don't really have to go to church to be a Christian."

- "Even though he is not a Christian, I think God wants me to be with him. Maybe God will use me to bring him into the Kingdom."

- "I listen to that music because of the beat, not the words."

- "We are both mature adults; we can live together and be strong. Besides, we're going to get married anyway."

- "There's nothing wrong with going out with the guys every now and then. I just hang out and socialize; I don't do the things they're doing."

- "We're just friends; she helps me out with the things I'm going through—things my wife and I are struggling with. She's a good listener."

- "It was just a little lie that didn't hurt anyone. I needed the business from them to make ends meet. What's the harm if no one gets hurt or knows?"

- "A couple of glasses of booze helps me to unwind each night. It's not that big a deal."

As you can see, the opportunities to walk outside the constraints of the wall are limitless. The Apostle Paul said,

"All things are lawful, but not all things are profitable."

—1 Corinthians 10:23, NASB

What he was saying is, yeah, we can do what we want, but when it is outside the limits God has set for us, we will have consequences, and we, in turn, limit our usefulness for God's purposes.

I am reminded of a story that I have used occasionally of a goldfish in his nice little bowl on the coffee table. One day the goldfish decided he was sick and tired of the hard glass walls of his bowl. He was tired of everyone always peeking in at him—tired of the confinement of his space. He decided he was going to make a way for himself and get out of this place once and for all.

He started swimming around and around faster and faster and then leaped up out of the water, over the side and onto the floor where he rapidly became aware of his mistake.

We are so often like this fish. We yearn to live and experience life. We think that somehow the constraints of the scripture hold us back from really living. But, in fact, the opposite is actually true. The bounds of the scripture actually give us the freedom to live life more abundantly.

You see God made us and He knows what is best for us. It's not to hold us back and make us miserable, but rather to protect us from ourselves, our nature, and the world. Remember the story of the Prodigal Son? The father knew his son would endure hardship and trouble in the world outside the protection of his home and family. His heart was ripped in two as he watched his son leave, knowing the pain he would endure in his rebellion.

Our Heavenly Father feels the same about us. He will not stop us from being rebellious and "experiencing life." He will just wait for us to come to our senses.

There have been several occasions that I have been tempted as bullets were flying and bombs exploding to get up on the roof, or climb up to the top of the wall and peer over to see the action. This thought goes away quickly as I remember that there are snipers all over just waiting to get a clear shot at us. Although the temptation to see is great, the knowledge of certain danger lurking on the other side is plenty enough incentive for me to remain in my sanctuary.

Remember, the enemy has a multitude of spiritual snipers just waiting for the child of God to wander off course and out from under the protective boundaries that God has established. Walk in the safety of the Lord Jesus and long for His presence and love, not the action outside the gate.

Until next week, walk straight, walk right and walk tall in God's ways!

Pastor Ryan
Ramadi, Iraq

Application:

Have you ever been tempted to travel outside the wall? Have you found yourself from time to time drawn by the action and thrill of what may lie on the other side? I think most of us have. It is important to remember during these times that God has placed certain limits and barriers in our lives, not for the purpose of holding us back from good things, but to protect us from bad things. In His perfect wisdom and knowledge He has lovingly placed safety nets for us to prevent us from the pitfalls that we and the enemy set before us. Remember, a moment outside the wall can result in a lifetime of consequences. What are God's limits for you? He reveals them to you day by day as you spend time in His Word. He not only show us limits, He also reveals to us the great freedom and liberty we have in Him. Allow His limits to set you free today!

Prayer:

Dear Jesus, as I consider those protections that You have placed in my life and those limits that tutor me, help me not to despise or resent them, but rather to look at them as tools that free me. Help me to always abide in Your presence and behind your walls as I consider each day what you have for my life. I surrender my will to You today completely.

In Jesus' Name I pray, Amen.

Day 11

Complacency Kills

"I know your deeds, that you are neither cold nor hot."

—Revelation 3:15

4 November 2004

All over Camp Blue Diamond you see signs that say, "Complacency Kills." This is a constant and sobering reminder that being ever vigilant is key to survival here on the battlefield. Many Marines, Sailors and Soldiers while in the relatively safe environment of the base camp have a tendency to get into a routine and go about their business and daily tasks in an almost automated manner.

What this does is produce a sense of decreased awareness and urgency, and it certainly lessens your awareness of your surroundings. I don't have to tell you that in this environment it can mean the difference between life and death.

Let me give you several examples of things we must constantly be prepared for:

- When the enemy attacks us with rockets or mortars, the alarms go off and people are to run to cover and put their protective body armor on to protect against shrapnel. Many are very slow in doing this because very few actually hit close to anything on base. After some time, there is the danger that people won't take the alarms as seriously as they should, and rather than run to cover, they walk or stroll or don't take cover at all. This can result in warriors being out in the open when the second or third round of incoming hits, and consequently run the risk of being wounded, and one, several months ago, was actually killed. To ignore warnings is bad business in the war zone.

- While out on patrol in town or doing raids on houses or buildings not to be keenly aware of surroundings can be disastrous. The moment you take your guard down or are not 100% vigilant is the moment the enemy will get a shot in or get you from behind. Having a situational awareness at all times is crucial.

- While manning a vehicle checkpoint on the roads in and out of the city to not be always watchful and alert of those vehicles approaching can mean disaster for the whole team. Being on the lookout for the warning indicators prior to a vehicle driving up is a must.

These are just a few examples of circumstances that can have deadly or harmful consequences when one does not always stay on the alert and falls into complacency. God reminded me as I thought on this topic that from a spiritual standpoint we run the same risk of harmful and devastating consequences to our spiritual health and our effectiveness for the Kingdom when we fall prey to complacency.

The scripture declares in Peter 2:8: *"Be self-controlled and alert. Your enemy the devil prowls around like a roaring lion looking for someone to devour."*

The image that the Apostle Peter is portraying is striking. Consider the great herds of animals on the African plains. There are many kinds, many sizes, but all have one thing in common. They travel in numbers for safety. The lion lurks around the edges of the watering holes and feeding grounds, hiding in the tall grass, waiting—waiting for just the right time, just the right animal. That is the one who is sick, young, old, weak, or who just plain loses track of the heard while grazing in a nice spot. In a burst of explosive speed, before the unsuspecting animal knows what has happened, 500 pounds of lion is upon them, and that is the end…

Jesus also warned of this type of danger as it pertains to His followers and their relationship to Him when He warned the Church of Laodicea:

> *"I know your deeds, that you are neither cold nor hot. I wish you were either one or the other! So, because you are lukewarm—neither hot nor cold—I am about to spit you out of My mouth."*
> —Revelation 3:15-16

At first glance this almost does not make sense for Jesus to say He wishes we were either cold or hot. Why would Jesus want us to be cold? Many scholars believe the answer to this lies in the culture and location known to the Laodiceans.

There were no natural water sources in the town and so, consequently, great troughs made of stone, placed upon stands, ran from the water source many miles away to the city bringing it water. This trough was open to the sun and contained many minerals and sediments. By the time the water reached the city, any unsuspecting visitor who unknowingly took a drink from this trough would spew out the lukewarm foul tasting water.

Jesus' desire for them to be either hot or cold came in contrast to the foul water in the trough. It was a reference to the well-known hot mineral baths not far away which were healing and soothing, along with the cool spring water which was the source for the water trough which would be refreshing and rejuvenating to a weary soul. His desire for us is to be a healing and refreshing comfort to those in need and hurting, this in contrast to the nasty, nauseating water from the trough before it was purified.

The picture is striking and clear. We must always be vigilant and aware, always ready to minister to those in need and never allow ourselves to fall into a complacent spiritual condition—a condition which in no way pleases our Lord, and certainly is of no benefit to the Kingdom of God.

Until next week, stay vigilant and aware and be constantly refreshed in the Living Water. Take that Living Water to those dying in the desert, to those who are downcast, and to those who have lost hope. Be HOT or COLD!

Walking in His grace,
Pastor Ryan
Ramadi, Iraq

Application:

Sometimes in life it is tempting to let our guard down. This usually happens when things are going well and all seems to be right. Just before the lion springs from his hiding place upon the unsuspecting gazelle, all seems peaceful and quiet. It is when this sense of calm sets in that we take our eyes off the road for just a few seconds. It only takes a second for the lion to be on top of the gazelle and seconds to swerve off the road. Resist the tendency we all have to take our eyes off God, to read the Word less and to pray less when all is well. We can find ourselves in real trouble, really fast!

Prayer:

Lord, help us to remain always with our eyes fixed upon You, whether good times or bad. In all areas and seasons of life may we always have a sense of urgency in our devotions and prayer life and a strong sense of focus on those things that matter most. Father, we know that when we seek first Your Kingdom that all other things seem to fade away. We pray Lord that You would empower us by Your Holy Spirit to live victoriously and keep YOU first.

In Your Holy Name we pray, Amen.

Day 12

The Battle Belongs to the Lord

"You must not fear them, for the LORD your God Himself fights for you."
—Deuteronomy 3:22

11 November 2004

Be encouraged in your spirit, for the Lord fights for you. This is not a fight of flesh and blood only, but of powers and principalities. Many critics of the war on terror have said that all we have done is open ourselves up to greater danger of terrorism by taking Saddam Hussein out of power and invading Iraq. My response to that is nothing could be further from the truth. The scripture declares to us in Daniel 2:

> *"Blessed be the name of God forever and ever, For wisdom and might are His. And He changes the times and the seasons; He removes kings and raises up kings; He gives wisdom to the wise And knowledge to those who have understanding. He reveals deep and secret things; He knows what is in the darkness, And light dwells with Him."*
> —Daniel 2:20-22

Daniel was praising God for giving him the interpretation to Nebuchadnezzar's dream when all of the magicians, astrologers and Chaldeans could not. Although Daniel was speaking of a specific victory God had given to him and his companions, the wisdom of Daniel's words reaches far beyond that. It is God's divine purpose and prerogative to appoint and to cast down kingdoms and kings. The wicked and evil kings will not stand forever.

Such is the case with Nebuchadnezzar whose heart was not changed though he witnessed God's power and wisdom through the interpretation of two of his dreams and the supernatural deliverance of Daniel's three companions Shadrach (Hananiah), Meshach (Mishael), and Abed-nego (Azariah) from the fiery furnace.

God will go to great lengths with great mercy and perseverance to reach us in our rebellion. The king had seen many wonders and the display of God's power right before his very eyes, and yet he did not humble himself. (See Daniel 4:28-34)

It is not a coincidence that in the same place today, Babylon, the former ruling king, who has declared himself to be the reincarnate Nebuchadnezzar of old, has defied the living God through his barbaric acts, his murderous ways and his arrogant defiance of the laws of God.

Daniel declared in verse 22 that God *"reveals deep and secret things; He knows what is in the darkness and light dwells with Him."* Our attack on Saddam's regime in Iraq and subsequent liberation of the people has not caused the United States and the rest of the world to be at greater risk for terrorism as some have claimed. Rather, it has had the effect of pulling back the veil and exposing the truth of the evil that existed here.

Saddam's tight grip on the country for years and years has buffered and covered the true face of the evil that was occurring here. God has in effect, through the agent of this President and the military, "shown a light in the darkness," exposing every evil deed. That which we now see has always been here and is only now being seen for what it is.

Nebuchadnezzar defied the living God and was humbled. Likewise, Saddam Hussein has done the same and has now been brought into an accounting for his deeds. The backlash of insurgency and foreign fighters that we see was what was revealed with the light and has existed all along.

How long do you think it would have been before they ended up on our front doorstep in the United States and other countries? Not long. We are not invincible and especially not when we as a nation begin to turn our backs on our rich Godly heritage and throw God's grace aside for a righteousness of our own—a moral relativity and a forsaking of the God who gave us our liberty and blessings as a country.

9/11 was a wake up call for all Americans. God has given us one more chance to take a stand for righteousness and for His ways. We made our voice known on election day and reelected God's chosen man. We also made our voice known in every state, denying attempts to re-define marriage. We must continue to stand as God's people and as "One Nation Under God."

We have seen many casualties over the past four days. I have moved more than 200 wounded Marines, Soldiers and Sailors in the past 72 hours alone. We have had more than 20 killed in action. The cost is high, but the stakes are high.

My brothers and sisters continue to shed their blood on this battlefield believing in the concept of a free America and a chance for all to live in freedom, free from tyranny—not just our children but also the children of Iraq and Afghanistan and many other places.

Lift up a shout to the living God for all of us and declare that we will not surrender one inch of ground to the enemy ever again! When you lay your head down at night, thank God for the mercy and the freedom He has granted to all of us.

When you consider the purpose for *your* life consider *God's* purpose for your life instead. When you get into your car and drive to work, give God thanks that you don't have to worry about a suicide bomber driving into you or your family.

When you think of those who have given the ultimate sacrifice, shed a tear for them and pray for their families. Take a stand for God knowing that He stands for you. Believe that revival in our land is possible, and no longer let your voice go unheard. We have all spoken from the battlefield; we have all taken a stand.

Sleep well and peaceful tonight knowing that we are standing the watch. We will always stand the watch. You do your part and stand watch over our spirits as you faithfully lift us up in prayer. Thank You God for another chance for our Nation and our people, may we never let our guard down again.

Faithfully standing the watch,
Pastor Ryan
Ramadi, Iraq

Application:

So many times we find that it is easier to not say something when we see injustice and wrong acts being committed around us. It's easier just to get along and fit in than to rock the boat. It may be easier to live this way, but it is not what God commands us to do. We are to be salt and light at all times. We are the preservative in our workplace, schools, communities and family. God has called us to stand firm even after we have done all we can do. Don't be swayed or allow the fear of man to cloud your judgment or dissuade you from standing up for the truth and doing what is right.

Prayer:

Lord, so many times I find that I am afraid to stand up for the right things. I confess that I am afraid of what people will think of me or that they will make fun of me or reject me. Lord, please remove my fear of what others think, and give me boldness and courage to stand up for Your Kingdom and for the name of Jesus. I need You Lord more than ever to fill me with Your Holy Spirit and empower me to make a difference in this world. I want my light to shine brightly in this dark world from this day forward.

In Jesus' Holy Name, Amen.

Day 13

Battlefield Salvation

"He has delivered us from the power of darkness and conveyed us into the kingdom of the Son of His love, in whom we have redemption through His blood, the forgiveness of sins."
—Colossians 1:13-14

19 November 2004

As I have been studying Paul's letter to the Romans the past week or so, God began to speak to me about salvation and gave me an example right here on the battlefield. The things He shows me and puts into my mind and heart as I spend time meditating and reading His Word always intrigue me.

Last night as I spent time with Him, He began to drop little snippets into my heart. I remember stumbling across a profound parallel to salvation and having a big smile on my face because I was so excited about what God was showing me. Hopefully, it will all come out well as I write this today.

As we know, salvation is both simple and complex. The message of salvation is so simple that a child can understand it, yet so complex that certain aspects of it have been debated by great scholars for nearly 2000 years. Paul talks about several aspects of salvation in his letter to the Romans. I would like to tie them to what I have seen here in Iraq.

Redemption

This is a term that Paul uses to describe that which Jesus did for us on the Cross. He set us free by satisfying the full requirement of the Law which demanded a sacrifice and the shedding of blood. Through this process, He broke the bond of sin which chained us and imprisoned us. This also includes the fact that there was nothing we could have done to deserve or merit this gift.

Likewise, the Iraqi people were under terrible bondage to a ruthless dictator and tyrant. They were, in fact, slaves to the rule of the land, powerless to free themselves. They were freely redeemed and set free by our throwing off this heavy yoke that was Saddam's regime.

While it is true that the people were free the moment that Saddam's government was overthrown and it is true that we are saved the moment we believe and confess Jesus as Lord and Savior, the work is not done for Iraq or for us.

> *"...even the righteousness of God, through faith in Jesus Christ, to all and on all who believe. For there is no difference; for all have sinned and fall short of the glory of God, being justified freely by His grace through the redemption that is in Christ Jesus..."*
>
> —Romans 3:22-24

> *"He has delivered us from the power of darkness and conveyed us into the kingdom of the Son of His love, in whom we have redemption through His blood, the forgiveness of sins."*
>
> —Colossians 1:13-14

Justification

Justification is a legal term that essentially means to be acquitted or declared right in the eyes of the law. This happens simultaneously with redemption for those who place their trust in Jesus Christ for salvation. God declares that we are righteous in His eyes based on the completed work of Jesus on the Cross. He attributes the righteousness of Christ to us and effectively says: "Not guilty."

This happened for the Iraqi people in May with the declaration of the Coalition Provisional Authority transferring legal authority back to the Iraqi people and giving them their sovereignty. They were declared legally a sovereign and free country with the authority to make their own decisions and choices as a nation.

In the eyes of the world, they have been legally declared right and legitimate based on the work and sacrifice of another. How wonderful is this gift of salvation and liberty!

> "...being justified freely by His grace through the redemption that is in Christ Jesus..."
> —Romans 3:24

Sanctification

This is a word which describes the ongoing process of change and purification that the Holy Spirit works in the life of each believer. Millard J. Erickson defines sanctification as "the continuing work of God in the life of a believer." The ultimate goal of God for each believer is for him or her to become more and more conformed to the image of Christ.

> "But we all, with unveiled face, beholding as in a mirror the glory of the Lord, are being transformed into the same image from glory to glory, just as by the Spirit of the Lord."
> —2 Corinthians 3:18

"...being confident of this very thing, that He who has begun a good work in you will complete it until the day of Jesus Christ..."

—Philippians 1:6

Likewise in Iraq, there is an ongoing process of transforming this country more and more into the image of a free and democratic nation—a nation where there is the freedom to vote, work and voice your opinion without fear or retribution. This process, as we are well aware of, is slow, painful and costly, while at the same time being joyful, purposeful and victorious.

For every uprising and pocket of defiance and resistance there are 20 or 30 victories for the people. Schools and hospitals and houses are being built every day; water and power is being restored. Security is slowly being restored as we train the Iraqi forces to defend themselves and their country.

Over 2,000 Iraqi troops fought valiantly and bravely along side U.S. troops in Fallujah this past week. This was not the case in April when we first went into Fallujah. Where once there were no people on the streets for fear of thugs and insurgents, there are now families out and children playing.

The sanctification process in the life of a believer is likewise painful and difficult at times, and we go through trials and tribulation. But we also experience many victories as God purifies us and sets us free from old habits and vices that once held us captive. Soon this process will be complete in Iraq, and ultimately in each believer.

Glorification

Our salvation is complete the day we enter into glory with Jesus. What a day that will be! He will give us a new body that is not corrupted by the flesh and the world. Glorification is the end result of sanctification in our life—the ultimate goal you might say. Our home is not of this world but in heaven.

> *"For we know that the whole creation groans and labors with birth pangs together until now. Not only that, but we also who have the first fruits of the Spirit, even we ourselves groan within ourselves, eagerly waiting for the adoption, the redemption of our body. For we were saved in this hope, but hope that is seen is not hope; for why does one still hope for what he sees? But if we hope for what we do not see, we eagerly wait for it with perseverance."*
> —Romans 8:22-25

The Holy Spirit is a kind of "deposit" in the life of believers foreshadowing the future glory that we will one day enjoy with God. In Iraq, there will be a glorification in the near future. There will come a day when the deposit of all the work our forces and the Iraqi forces have done to root out the insurgency will come to a wonderful and glorious conclusion. There will be safety and security for every citizen, freedom from fear and terror, and the right to have a voice in electing those who will lead the country.

What an awesome day that will be—one that no one in this country has tasted, but soon will experience. Praise God for His continuing work of salvation and purification in our lives as believers and for the process that is working for the good of the people of Iraq!

From the Battlefield,
Pastor Ryan
Ramadi, Iraq

Application:

Many times in our walk with the Lord we find that we fall short of perfection. In fact, I would venture to say we fall short more than we hit the mark. The enemy loves to remind us of this fact and discourage us by planting lies and deception in our minds. He loves to tell us that we are not really Christians because real Christians would never do what we have done, or think what we have thought. He is a liar and the father of all lies. Don't let him get to you. Stand on the promise of God's Word when you fall short. "If we confess our sins, He is faithful and just to forgive us *our* sins and to cleanse us from all unrighteousness." 1 John 1:9. Remember, we are being molded and shaped more and more into the image of Christ each day. This process occurs over our entire lifetime, not overnight.

Prayer:

Lord, I find myself discouraged many times when I fail You. Sometimes I feel like in order to be a Christian I have to be perfect always. I know that there will be times that I will miss Your mark, and today I ask You to strengthen me so that my failures become less and less each day. I want to be more like You and less like me with every passing moment. I ask You Lord to create a clean heart and mind in me as I commit my works to You each day. My desire, Lord, is to truly be holy as You are holy. Thank You Lord Jesus for hearing my prayer today.

In Your precious Name, Amen.

Day 14

Spiritual Pre-Deployment Check List

"This is the inventory of the tabernacle, the tabernacle of the Testimony, which was counted according to the commandment of Moses, for the service of the Levites, by the hand of Ithamar, son of Aaron the priest."

—Exodus 38:21

23 November 2004

We are the Temple, or Tabernacle of the Holy Spirit. As such, it is important that we have a complete inventory of those things necessary for our service to God in the Tabernacle—which is every believer. Each part and piece has a distinct use and function necessary to carry out God's Will. We, too, have many things that must be accounted for and in place in our life which are necessary for our service to God.

In my years in the military I have deployed numerous times, not only full scale deployments for combat operations or war fighting, but training operations as well. In my experience one thing I have found to be very true is that attention to detail and preparation is crucial to success. Prior to leaving there is much that must take place to ensure a "ready" state. Along with this list, God has shown me that much in the Christian life parallels this process of preparation to ensure spiritual success.

Deployment Task #1

Begin to prepare yourself and your family mentally and emotionally for the time that will be spent away from one another. This is very important as this aspect of military life tears many families apart.

Spiritual Insight #1

We have the heavy responsibility to prepare our families and ourselves spiritually for a life in Christ. We must give our children the very best opportunity in life and impress upon them the importance of serving Christ in their own life. We must be that leader in the family who not only says, but does! This means time in the Word and prayer together as well as individually.

Deployment Task #2

It is crucial that all life insurance be current and completed before you leave. Life on the battlefield is unpredictable and dangerous. It is important to ensure that your family is taken care of should something happen to you.

Spiritual Insight #2

Making sure that your eternal life insurance policy is in place should be our first order of business. Knowing that you belong to Christ and have made that commitment of faith by trusting in Jesus for eternal life is the foundation on which all other things must be built. Apart from knowing Christ, everything else is in vain.

Deployment Task #3

Make sure that your will is in place in the event of your passing. This is very important for ensuring that your belongings go where you want them to go, and do not get caught up in the legal system.

Spiritual Insight #3

Making sure that "God's Will" is in affect in your life is even more critical. Your will declares to the powers that be where you want your stuff to go should you die; God's will in our life shows the world Who our life belongs to.

Deployment Task #4

Be sure that you have a current power of attorney in a place so your spouse or other trustworthy person can carry on your financial and legal affairs while you are gone. Deployments often come with extended periods of isolation, making it impossible to do this for yourself.

Spiritual Insight #4

Surrender the "power of your will" over to the only "Trustworthy One!" You must relinquish the control of all areas of your life to the One who bought you with a price, the price of His own blood. Having His mighty Holy Spirit is what truly gives you the power to live a victorious life.

Deployment Task #5

Make sure all of your financial affairs are current and necessary commitments taken care of. This is closely related to the Power of Attorney and having someone trustworthy to take care of these matters in your absence.

Spiritual Insight #5

Are you storing up treasures in heaven and being a wise steward of what God has entrusted to you? Are you giving to the Kingdom of God for the furtherance of the Gospel? Are you trusting God with your finances and giving Him what is already His? There is no better way to have your finances in order than to do it according to "God's Economy." Trust your finances to the Banker Who always gives a return on your deposit!

Deployment Task #6

You must do a complete inventory of your 782 gear and sea bag to make sure you have everything necessary to do your job for an extended period of time away from home. This includes making sure your war gear is functioning, fits properly and is all accounted for. Forgetting something can be very bad, especially when you reach for something and find that it is not there. Likewise, not bringing enough changes of clothing for the trip can wind up causing you to offend everyone around you!

Spiritual Insight #6

You must do an inventory of your spiritual life to ensure that you are doing the things that God has called you to do, making sure that you prioritize your life in a way that surrenders to God's purpose, discarding those things you don't need that have no benefit to the Kingdom of God, replacing them with those things that matter most. You must ensure that you have nothing sinful or anything in competition in the place that only God should have in our life.

Deployment Task #7

All troops deploying must ensure that all their immunizations and physical exams are complete. This is preventative medicine in case we come into contact with some nasty disease often found in other parts of the world.

Spiritual Insight #7

The greatest spiritual preventive measures we can take are to make sure we are walking closely with our Lord at all times, staying close to the vine that supplies the branches with nourishment. This will ensure our spiritual health and protect us against unseen attacks by the spiritual viruses of this world.

Deployment Task #8

Get your weapon from the armory. This includes not only obtaining it, but also cleaning it, maintaining it, and making sure it functions properly. In addition to this, prior to deployment, everyone must go to the shooting range to make sure we know how to use our weapon.

Spiritual Insight #8

Spiritually this means we must be able to wield the power of the Sword of the Spirit at all times. We must know God's Word inside and out and be ready at anytime to deploy it against the attack of the enemy.

Deployment Task #9

Ensure that you are proficient in your regular job specialty. This includes training and courses to keep your skills current and sharp. For example, if you are a combat medic such as I am, training in all the latest trauma and emergency medical procedures for the battlefield is paramount. For Marines or Soldiers this might include mechanic, flight crew or radio and communications training. These must be current and the individual must be able to do the job in every environment and in any circumstance.

Spiritual Insight #9

Being proficient in your job as a Christian is a must before you go into battle. Your knowledge of scripture, its application to your life, and your prayer life should be finely tuned so that you may be truly effective in this mission. You should be ready at all times to preach the Good News of Jesus Christ.

Deployment Task #10

Make sure you have your buddy's back. Part of what makes Marines and Soldiers so dedicated on the battlefield is knowing beyond a shadow of doubt that the guy next to you has your back, and if necessary, will lay his life down for you. American troops have lived by this code for as long as our military has existed.

Spiritual Insight #10

Do you have your neighbor's back? Are you fulfilling the great commandment to love your neighbor as yourself? Do you esteem others more than yourself? Part of loving those around you is telling them the truth about Jesus Christ. Greater love has no man than this than to lay down one's life for his friend. My prayer each day is: "Lord, lead me to at least on person today that I can share Your love with."

If you can go down your spiritual checklist and check off these things, you should be ready to deploy into the service God has for you. Remember, you are the Temple of the Holy Spirit, and in God's Temple, everything must be in place and ready.

My prayer is that when you do your spiritual inventory, God will help you to identify anything that needs to be rearranged, replaced or discarded for a life fully prepared to impact this world for Jesus Christ.

From the Battlefield,
Pastor Ryan
Ramadi, Iraq

Application:

Most of us would never go on a journey without at least doing a mental checklist or inventory of what we need to bring and what needs to be done prior to leaving. Those who do not take these necessary steps find that inevitably something is left out or forgotten, leaving one in an uncomfortable or precarious place. If we take such care for a short vacation or trip, why do we not conduct an even more necessary list of checks and balances in our spiritual journey? After all, this journey is for life!

Prayer:

Lord, Your Holy Word is a great manual and checklist for my life with You. Help me to take stock in Your Word and apply the life giving principles to my daily journey. I thank You that You loved me so much that You sent Jesus to die for me. I thank You that You thought so much of me that You gave me Your one and only Son to serve as a living example of those things that I should do in my own life to remain close to You. Help me to ensure that I have every box checked and that all systems are go.

In the glorious Name of Christ my Lord, Amen.

Day 15

He Has Prepared a Place for Me

"Behold, I stand at the door and knock. If anyone hears My voice and opens the door, I will come in to him and dine with him, and he with Me."

—Revelation 3:20

26 November 2004

Today, on this day after Thanksgiving, I am feeling many emotions ranging from sorrow and sadness to joy and thankfulness. I am sad and sorrowful for the families who will find out about the loss of their loved ones on the battlefield on Thanksgiving Day. There is sadness in my spirit anytime they have to be told that their husband, brother, son, or daddy will not be coming home. I wish there were some way that I could bring comfort to them. That is not something I can do from where I sit, but I can pray for them—and I will.

There is sadness inside me after talking with my wife and realizing just how much I miss her and the family. She said something to me that I am not ashamed to say made me cry; yet at the same time, it filled my heart with love and warmth. She said, "Ryan, I set a place for you at the table."

My heart was bursting in my chest, and I was so thankful to God for giving me the perfect wife—the most precious and cherished thing I have this side of heaven. This meant more to me than anything she could have said.

It also made me stop and consider all that God has done for us as His children—the many blessings that each one of us possess in our lives. Even those of us who do not have much more than the shirt on our back are rich in spirit if we know the Living God. God has given us the best gift that could ever be given, His Son!

He has granted us freedom to worship and freedom to give our kids the best chance at life. He has placed us in a right standing with Himself through the shed blood of Jesus. If you were to sit down right now and think of all that you have to be thankful for, I am sure you could fill several pages of a notebook.

I am thankful for the opportunity to serve the men and women who are fighting for freedom, to make a difference for them when they fall—to not only pray for them as their name comes to my desk, but to carry the heavy responsibility of getting them help as quickly as possible. I know that what I do directly impacts each and every person on this battlefield, especially those who are wounded.

God has so blessed me with this place and position, a position that carries heavy responsibility. But it is not my own power or efforts which make the real difference. It is the prayers of so many around the globe who hold my arms up as the battle wages on. I am aware each day of the strength that God gives me through the prayers of so many. I am thankful for all of you.

God has set a place at His table for each of us. He has prepared the banquet, and each of us is invited as His special guest. With an invitation such as this, what a sad thing it would be to not show up. To be invited to His table for eternity, to dine with Him and sit in His presence—there is no greater opportunity than this. Yet, so many will not show up; so many will not be ready when the call comes.

I think of the words of my wife, "I have set a place for you." If there were anything in my ability or power that would have allowed me to sit down at the place that had been set for me, I would have been there. I would have sat with my wife and family and enjoyed that moment.

While this was true for me, there is nothing that prevents the rest of us from sitting down at the place that God has prepared for us. It is simply a matter of accepting the invitation.

> *"Then He said to him, 'A certain man gave a great supper and invited many, and sent his servant at supper time to say to those who were invited, 'Come, for all things are now ready.' But they all with one accord began to make excuses. The first said to him, 'I have bought a piece of ground, and I must go and see it. I ask you to have me excused.' And another said, 'I have bought five yoke of oxen, and I am going to test them. I ask you to have me excused.' Still another said, 'I have married a wife, and therefore I cannot come.'"*
>
> —Luke 14:16-20

You will notice that each of the three people mentioned by Jesus had no valid excuse. The invitation for the banquet would have gone out long before the occasion, leaving plenty of time for the guests to plan and make sure their schedule was open. In fact, in the Hebrew culture it was a great insult to the host for the guests not to show up.

There really is no reason for any of us to miss out on what God has prepared for us. His invitation has gone out long in advance. Could there be anything more important than showing up at this feast?

My heart was broken being away from my wife and family on this Thanksgiving Day, but know that nothing will stop me from attending God's Banquet. He invites each of us individually. Consider these Words from God:

"Behold, I stand at the door and knock. If anyone hears My voice and opens the door, I will come in to him and dine with him, and he with Me."

—Revelation 3:20

To share an intimate time of fellowship with the Lord Jesus Christ is to share in the greatest honor of all. The Lord's most intimate time with his disciples came around the table of fellowship. Here His heart was opened completely to them. Here He extended one of the greatest acts of love this side of the cross.

Not only did He wash the feet of His disciples, He washed the feet of Judas his betrayer as well. Until the very last moment, He extended His love and invitation for Judas to turn back to Him. He does the same for all of us. He is not willing that any should perish but that all would accept His invitation to spend eternity with Him.

As I sit on the battlefield with my brothers and sisters in arms, I am reminded of the many who would do me harm outside these walls if given the opportunity. As I pray tonight and consider my many blessings, my prayer of thanksgiving to God will be:

"The LORD is my shepherd; I shall not want.
He makes me to lie down in green pastures;
He leads me beside the still waters.
He restores my soul;
He leads me in the paths of righteousness
For His name's sake.
Yea, though I walk through the valley of the shadow of death,
I will fear no evil; For You are with me;

Your rod and Your staff, they comfort me.
You prepare a table before me in the presence of my
    enemies;
You anoint my head with oil; My cup runs over.
Surely goodness and mercy shall follow me
All the days of my life;
And I will dwell in the house of the LORD Forever."

—Psalm 23

May your prayer be likewise as you continue to thank God for the many blessings of life. May you always remember His goodness and mercy all the days of your life, and may you do all you can to make sure that you and all you know are at the Lord's banquet. Can there be anything more important?

From the Battlefield,
Pastor Ryan
Ramadi, Iraq

Application:

I wonder how we would change our perspective on life if we knew Jesus would be returning next week? I wonder if we would have a greater urgency in telling others about Him? If I knew where I could get one million dollars for free with no strings attached and that anyone else could get a million dollars for free too, I wonder how many people I would tell? In essence, we have something so much more valuable than any money or object, and yet we have no urgency to share it with others. Jesus has prepared a place for all of us at His table; make it your purpose and life's goal to bring as many friends as you possibly can with you to dinner!

Prayer:

Lord, so many times I let life get in the way of what I should really be doing. Help me to put first things first each and everyday. Help me to have greater boldness in telling others about You and inviting them to come with me to dinner at Your house. Help me to have a greater Kingdom perspective rather than my own limited worldly view. Please lead me to at least one person today with whom I can share Your love.

In Your Holy Name I pray, Amen.

Day 16

The Greatest Weapon

"The Word of God is living and powerful, and sharper than any two-edged sword, piercing even to the division of soul and spirit, and of the joints and marrow, and is a discerner of the thoughts and intents of the heart.
—Hebrews 4:12

3 December 2004

Today as I write, God has given me another vivid illustration from the battlefield. It seems that around every corner there is yet another striking parallel to our lives in the Spirit. The longer I am here, and the more I read and study God's Word, the more I have come to realize that everything about warfare and combat in the physical realm has its close kin in the spiritual realm.

In my daily duties and as I walk around the camp and visit with Marines and Soldiers, one thing I have noticed over and over is the great care and attention to detail that all troops give their weapons. Each morning as I get off the night shift and walk back to my room, I see scores of warriors with their weapons broken down into pieces, spending great time and energy ensuring cleanliness and proper functioning.

Those who go out on patrols every day are even more diligent in this effort. All Marines, Sailors and Soldiers have personal weapons that include M-16 rifles, shotguns, or pistols. The expectation is that they will be cleaned everyday. However, although this is the normal expectation from the chain of command, most do not find it difficult to find the motivation to care for their weapon.

In fact, most realize that if their weapon is dirty or not oiled properly, when it really matters, it will malfunction. This is motivation enough for those who place their lives on the line each day.

In addition to the personal weapons, there are the larger mounted 50 caliber machine guns and Mark–19 grenade launchers that demand this same level of care and attention. In this environment, your weapon is your best friend and is sometimes the only thing between you and certain harm or even death.

Regardless of what specialty training a Marine has, their primary function is as a rifleman. As a matter of fact, one of the Marine Corps' sayings is "Every Marine is a rifleman." As this saying suggests, the greatest responsibility on the battlefield for Marines is to not only know their weapons, but to keep them ready to go at all times.

As a matter of fact, most soldiers I have met can break an M-16 down in less than 30 seconds and name every part. And, most can do it blindfolded! Each knows his or her weapon so intimately that even when disassembled he or she can immediately determine what is and what is not a part of that weapon—a critical aspect of life on the battlefield.

This brought to my mind the similar duty and need that we as Christians have with our weapon, the Word of God. It is critical that we have a detailed knowledge of all the parts of this powerful weapon.

We should know our weapon so well that even when Satan breaks it down deceptively as He did with Jesus, we should immediately be able to identify what is and what is not the truth of God's Word. It is sometimes the only thing we have that stands between us and certain spiritual danger or death.

An example of this can be found in the philosophy of the Royal Canadian Mounted Police. In identifying counterfeit money, they do not spend time studying counterfeit money; rather they study closely the genuine article so that anything counterfeit that presents itself to them, they immediately know the difference.

Jesus Himself wielded the mighty power of this weapon when combating Satan while in the wilderness.

> *"And the devil said to Him, "If You are the Son of God, command this stone to become bread." But Jesus answered him, saying, "It is written, "Man shall not live by bread alone, but by every word of God."*
>
> —Luke 4:3-4

In it are the very words of life for all of us.

> *"For I am not ashamed of the gospel of Christ, for it is the power of God to salvation for everyone who believes, for the Jew first and also for the Greek."*
>
> —Romans 1:16

It gives us understanding and wisdom.

> *"The entrance of Your words gives light; It gives understanding to the simple."*
>
> —Psalm 119:130

It keeps us pure and far from sin.

> *"Your word I have hidden in my heart, That I might not sin against You."*
>
> —Psalm 119:11

God's Word is the "tool of our trade" as Christians. Every experience, event, opinion and word must be measured and weighed against the standard of God's Word. In the impressive list of armor in Ephesians 6, our weapon, the Sword of the Spirit is the only piece that is offensive in nature. All other parts are to protect and preserve the person of God, but the Sword of the Spirit is that which is used to inflict damage on the kingdom of the enemy. It is that which is the very revelation of Jesus Christ Himself.

If knowing and seeing how important our personal weapons are on the battlefield, can our spiritual weapon be any less important? If a weapon of steel and plastic can avail so much in the physical setting of the battlefield, can a weapon of the Spirit yield any less in the spiritual battles that are waged around us?

If a burst of automatic rounds of lead can push back an enemy of flesh and blood, how much more can a burst of God's powerful Word bring results for the kingdom of God that is not of flesh and blood. As you consider today the war that we are engaged in here in Iraq, think also of the war which rages around all of us each day.

"For we do not wrestle against flesh and blood, but against principalities and powers..."
—Ephesians 6:12

Nothing that we can do in the flesh will advance the spiritual battle lines, only that which is done in the Spirit. Commit today to become an expert with this weapon that you possess for it may be that one-day it is all that stands between you and a relentless enemy. For it is sure that our enemies never rest on this battlefield, and know too that the enemy of our soul is tireless.

The good news is that when we wield the mighty power of the Sword of the Spirit of the Living God, truly, no weapon formed against us can prosper!

From the Battlefield,
Pastor Ryan
Ramadi, Iraq

Application:

Everything about being a Christian comes back to one thing—the Word of God. It is the source document which gives us detailed blueprints for living the Christian life. It is the owner's manual for the correct manner of living. As any builder or architect will tell you, if you deviate from the plans, the result will be less than ideal. Yet, so many Christians do not have a clue what the Bible really says. They know a few verses here and there but really have no idea why they believe what they believe. It is the most effective weapon we have against the enemy, and yet we find that many of us are ineffective in using it. This should not be. We should know the Word of God inside and out and return to the scriptures for answers to all of life's problems. Dig into the meat of the Word today.

Prayer:

Heavenly Father, I come before You this day in humility and faith, asking You to give me a renewed hunger and thirst for Your Holy Word. I realize that apart from Your Words of life there is no truth, and deception will follow me. Help me Lord to realize that if something does not stack up against the truth of Your Word that I am to reject it completely. I ask You to increase my knowledge and wisdom through Your Word and to help me to have it written on the tablets of my heart that I might not sin against You.

This I pray in Your Son Jesus' Name, Amen.

Day 17

Armed with the Truth

And you shall know the truth, and the truth shall make you free.

—John 8:31-32

10 December 2004

I found it amazing that every time we hit a target in the city of Fallujah, there happened to be a wedding, funeral, or hospital in the same location. Dozens of women, children, and elderly people were wounded or killed each time we attacked a suspected insurgent hideout.

Could we really be that sloppy and reckless with our intelligence? Was it possible that each attack coincidently found its mark during one of these social events in the city killing dozens of innocent civilians?

This is what the media was broadcasting from within Fallujah for months leading up to Operation Phantom Fury in November 2004 when 10,000 United States troops and more than 2,000 Iraqi troops toppled the insurgent stronghold of Fallujah.

I sat in the Command Operations Center and saw the intelligence and the planning and execution of each of these missions; I also saw the media stories that were more than ridiculous, and they made me angry.

The propaganda that came out of the city with each attack was casting a false light and twisted perception of what was truly happening. We would watch the attack from start to finish and then 45 minutes later see a fabricated news story. Half of the battle in Iraq was the media war; the truth was usually far from that which was reported.

The amazing thing was that once we took control of the hospital on the outskirts of the city, the negative propaganda stopped. When you shine a light into the darkness, the darkness disappears.

The same is true about our life as believers. We have a master manipulator and liar in the father of lies, Satan. The scripture declares this about him:

> *He was a murderer from the beginning, and does not stand in the truth, because there is no truth in him. When he speaks a lie, he speaks from his own resources, for he is a liar and the father of it."*

—John 8:44

What is it about the truth that is so difficult for us humans to grasp? We find it hard to tell the truth about even simple and silly things. As kids we can remember telling little white lies about breaking something in the house. At that stage it's kind of cute because your parents watched from around the corner as you broke the vase or tracked the mud in the house and then they see you adamantly deny what they just watched.

It's funny, but we sometimes still act as we did when we were children when it comes to hiding our sins from our Heavenly Father. When you think about this it almost seems silly because we know He sees everything we do. He even knows beforehand what we will do. There is nothing that is hidden from His view:

> *"You have set our iniquities before You, Our secret sins in the light of Your countenance."*

—Psalm 90:8

When the light of the United States and coalition forces shinned in the city of Fallujah, the reality of what was truly occurring in the city came to the world's eyes. The horrible torture chambers, dungeons, and stockpiles of weapons were clearly seen for the first time. When the light of Jesus Christ shines in our life no darkness can remain. He sets us free from destruction, and we are free indeed.

Our reputation is what people think of us. Our character is who we truly are when we are alone with God. The goal should be to have these two people meet and become the same person—the same in private that we are around others.

Jesus demands nothing less than integrity and uprightness in our walk with Him. He has called us to be holy as He is holy—to walk upright before God and man in all we do and say.

Remember, the world is watching us to see our conduct the same way they were watching the events in Iraq and Fallujah. We preach a sermon each day with our actions and words. What will the gospel be today according to you?

From the Battlefield,
Pastor Ryan
Ramadi, Iraq

Application:

I heard someone once say that there are two main reasons why people don't come to church: They don't know a Christian or they DO know a Christian! That is pretty sad when you think of it. We must do a better job of representing our Lord to the world. When we are a bad witness we reinforce the world's perception that the church is full of hypocrites. We go to church on Sunday and then live like the devil the rest of the week. Another saying I've heard is that a hypocrite is someone who is not him or herself during the week. I think that is wrong. I believe they are actually themselves during the week and pretending on Sundays. Are you a pretender?

Prayer:

Lord, I find it very hard at times to walk the walk—the true walk of faith. I am mindful today of a song that asks, "what if I stumble, what if I fall....what if I make fools of us all." Lord, more than anything in the world I want to honor You in my life and desire to never bring shame to Your name. Please help me Lord to walk in pureness of heart and in Godly character in all that I do. Help me to honor You with every aspect of my life.

In Your Name, Amen.

Day 18

One in Christ

"For as the body is one and has many members, but all the members of that one body, being many, are one body, so also is Christ."

—1 Corinthians 12:12

14 December 2004

God has been showing me the power that we have in the Body of Christ when we are a united body of believers. The Christians here on the battlefield have mainly two things in common: we all find ourselves in the midst of a war, and we have one chapel with one service where all of the Protestant faiths worship.

We have three chaplains who share the pulpit, and all are from different denominational backgrounds. One is Christian Reformed; one is Evangelical Lutheran Church of America; and the other is Evangelical Covenant Church of America. We also have a lay leader who helps who is Southern Baptist. And then there is my non-denominational, spirit filled background.

What this has given us is five different styles and approaches to the ministry on Blue Diamond. The thing that has been so wonderful to me as I experience and worship together with all types of people has been the amazing unity that we all share in the spirit.

There is every kind of faith group and tradition that you can imagine from Baptist to Pentecostal, Lutheran and

Methodist, Calvary Chapel and Presbyterian. We also have enjoyed sweet fellowship with the Royal Tongan Marines who are serving here with us. They are an amazing group of people from the Island Nation of Tonga which is rich in its faith in Christ.

We also have Iraqi, Indian, Jordanian and Philippinos who worship together with us. In addition there are civilians, Marines, Soldiers, Sailors and Airmen in attendance. The result has been a knitting together of all of our hearts and spirits into one body of believers. We all have different traditions and styles of worship, but the end result is a unity that is described in the early churches found in the Bible.

Jew and Gentile, Roman and Greek, slave and free, all worship the same God together. I believe Paul had this in mind when he spoke to the Corinthian Church and the Roman Church:

> *"For as the body is one and has many members, but all the members of that one body, being many, are one body, so also is Christ. For by one Spirit we were all baptized into one body—whether Jews or Greeks, whether slaves or free—and have all been made to drink into one Spirit. For in fact the body is not one member but many."*
>
> —1 Corinthians 12:12-14

> *"May the God who gives endurance and encouragement give you a spirit of unity among yourselves as you follow Christ Jesus, so that with one heart and mouth you may glorify the God and Father of our Lord Jesus Christ."*
>
> —Romans 15:5-6

Paul knew there were many obstacles to unity in the early church. The merging of Gentile believers with Jewish believers with their differing views on dietary laws and observance of traditions. Then there were those as well of high social and economic status with those who were slaves or poor. This merging together of such diverse groups was certainly an environment in which division and strife could take root. But as Paul explains,

> *"Therefore let us stop passing judgment on one another. Instead, make up your mind not to put any stumbling block or obstacle in your brother's way. As one who is in the Lord Jesus, I am fully convinced that no food is unclean in itself. But if anyone regards something as unclean, then for him it is unclean. If your brother is distressed because of what you eat, you are no longer acting in love. Do not by your eating destroy your brother for whom Christ died. Do not allow what you consider good to be spoken of as evil. For the kingdom of God is not a matter of eating and drinking, but of righteousness, peace and joy in the Holy Spirit, because anyone who serves Christ in this way is pleasing to God and approved by men."*
>
> —Romans 14:13-18

Living and worshiping together in unity and in submission to Christ in love is the highest and greatest responsibility that we have to our brothers and sisters in the Body of Christ. Dividing over non-essential items and those things that are merely a matter of opinion is contrary to the way of Christ.

While I acknowledge there are numerous and many expressions of worship and style within the Body, this should never be a hindrance to believers in Christ to love one another and to fellowship together.

I have found that I can enjoy the company of a brother or sister in Christ regardless of where they come from, what they look like or what denominational background they adhere to. We must yearn to break down barriers to loving one another, for such is the Kingdom of God.

There will be no such distinction in heaven; we will all worship the same God together in glory for eternity. Whether black or white, Baptist or Pentecostal, rich or poor, those who have been born again into the Body of Christ will enjoy this sweet fellowship together. Until next week, may the God of peace foster a spirit of unity in you and love for all who call upon the name of the Lord.

From the Battlefield,
Pastor Ryan
Ramadi, Iraq

Application:

Human nature is to judge people based upon outward appearances and what we perceive to be different or unusual. This is something that God desires to break in all of us. As was the case with David, God looked upon the inward man and the heart rather than the external appearance. In the Body of Christ many times we find that it is easier to divide and have no fellowship with those we don't agree with theologically. Sadly, most of these issues that divide Christians are nonessential matters that have no bearing on salvation or spiritual health. Most are a matter of comfort and personal preferences. The heart of God is for unity within His Body, and we can do much to help this process by refusing to engage in denominational criticism that only serves to tear others down.

Prayer:

Lord, today I take a stand for Your Kingdom and Your Body. I commit myself to look upon the heart rather than the differences and my perceived flaws in others. Help me Lord to see through Your eyes and to take on the mind of Christ as it pertains to the Kingdom of God. Never let me fall back into a critical spirit when dealing with my brothers and sisters. Help me to join You in uniting Your body rather than contribute to dividing it. I desire to be used as a Kingdom builder rather than working against it. Thank You Lord for using me for Your purposes this day.

In Jesus' Holy Name, Amen

Day 19

Hanging in the Balance

"My God, my God, why have you forsaken me?"

—Mark 15:34

17 December 2004

Something that I have been experiencing lately is an unusually bad case of homesickness. I am into my 4th month of deployment and as the days increase, so does my desire to be reunited with my wife. I have found that this feeling is compounded by the arrival of the holiday season of Thanksgiving and Christmas.

I am going to be very transparent in opening up my heart to share my inner feelings in this matter. God made Kellee and me for one another and when we were married we became one flesh, joined together as one in Christ. When that flesh is torn in two, the pain is great.

This deployment has been different from last year in that we have been able to email almost everyday and talk on the phone at least once a week. When you love someone so deeply and share all your dreams and life together, the absence of that person in your daily life, in daily conversations, and daily closeness with one another is very difficult to reconcile in your heart.

You come to depend on that person and become grafted together more and more with each passing day. You don't feel quite right until you are reunited.

While I am able to function in my job and daily tasks and I can minister God's love to others, there remains emptiness inside when I am away from her. Some might say, "But what about God, doesn't He give you a feeling of peace and fullness?" Yes He does.

He also joined me to my wife and put us together to experience life and the blessings of God together. I have joy in my heart and peace in the Lord no matter what my circumstances or how badly I miss my wife. He gives me that contentment to be at rest and trust Him in all things. Joy in spite of pain; joy in spite of loneliness; joy in spite of sadness.

Someone asked me one time what my greatest fear was. Considering that I was on the battlefield when I was asked this question one might think I answered with something having to do with the dangers of my environment and the perils of combat. My answer seemed to surprise this person and truthfully, even surprised me a bit. I said more than anything else, I feared being out of favor with God or not pleasing Him—to be in some way unable to connect with Him and sense His presence with me and in me.

This is not to say I don't fear other things. I fear not coming home to my wife and not seeing my family again. I sometimes worry about Kellee's safety and if she is sad or lonely. These are common feelings with long separations. However, above all else, I fear being far from God.

In the scripture, Jesus prayed in the Garden of Gethsemane prior to his betrayal and crucifixion. The Word says he was so distressed while in prayer that great drops of blood came from his body. He was under such intense pressure as a man facing a horrible death that His body of flesh reacted accordingly.

As a man He prayed *"Father, if You are willing, take this cup from Me."* But as God He prayed, *"Yet not My will, but Yours be done."* Jesus was crushed and heavy in spirit because of that which was to come, but even more than what He faced physically, He was bearing the knowledge of being separated from His Father for a time. Jesus says throughout the Gospels, *"I always do the will of My Father."*

More than any physical harm or trial He could face on earth, He could not bear the thought of not being one with His Heavenly Father or being out of intimate fellowship with Him. For Jesus, the greatest horror of the Cross was not the nails or the spears, it was, *"My God, My God, why have You forsaken Me."*

He was in such unity with the Father that for Him to be out of His presence, even for six hours as He hung on the tree, was simply unbearable, and yet because of His love for us, He endured this to completion. He simply could not leave it at "forsaken," he had to endure to "It is finished."

The fear I have of God and having such a strong desire to commune with Him is firmly implanted in my spirit and soul. The thought of being out of fellowship with Him is too unthinkable to endure.

When I can't talk to my wife on the phone for an extended time, or send messages over the email for several days, I feel like a lost puppy, sad and alone. When I don't talk to God for an extended period through prayer and His Word, I feel like a bone out of joint.

I experience emotional sadness and heart sickness when cut off from my wife. I experience spirit sickness and complete emptiness when I am out of fellowship with my God. To go days without my wife's comforting words is amazingly difficult, but to go days without my God's life giving Words is more than I can bear.

Have you felt yourself in this place before—hanging in the balance somewhere between sin and redemption—somewhere far removed from the grace and mercy of God because of busyness or neglect? Perhaps you have allowed old habits to creep up and overtake you, placing you out of God's favor and intimacy.

The Good News is that God is there if you will only turn around and run to Him. Jesus desires more than anything to dine with you and to welcome you into His presence. However, in the case of Jesus, as He became a sin offering for us, He was apart from God.

If you have found yourself in this place, God is eager to forgive you and welcome you back. He desires nothing more than for you to share oneness with Him and to have sweet fellowship with His children. Run to Him today!

From the Battlefield,
Pastor Ryan
Ramadi, Iraq

Application:

If you have ever found yourself in a place of distance from the Lord you know it is not a comfortable place to be. Yes, you may still be able to function in your different roles in life, but you are not really performing at your best. Think of it this way: If you were a high performance engine tuned to perfection, built for speed and power, you would want to perform at your optimal level. Now unplug one of your sparkplugs and fire on seven cylinders rather than eight. The result would be a choppy performance and a loss of power. The same is true of us when we are not firing on all spiritual cylinders!

Prayer:

Lord, at times I find myself feeling distant from You because of busyness or perhaps sin in my life. Help me Lord to do a Spiritual "tune-up" today and draw close to You once again. Renew the joy of my salvation and make my heart clean. Help me to do what is necessary to close the distance between my heart and Yours.

This I pray in the Name of Jesus, Amen.

Day 20

No Better Friend—No Worse Enemy

"He who believes in Him is not condemned; but he who does not believe is condemned already, because he has not believed in the name of the only begotten Son of God."

—John 3:18

24 December 2004

The 1st Marine Division has adopted as their motto "No better friend; No worse enemy" which is a slogan that has many implications. From the onset of Operation Iraqi Freedom, the Marines and Sailors of the 1st Marine Division have fought valiantly and honorably to bring freedom to the people of Iraq and rid this part of the world of terrorism that has threatened to spread throughout the world.

As most of us can see from the ongoing struggle with insurgency, this is not an easy task. In this part of the world there are many who oppose the presence of Americans and other westerners. There are many who oppose democracy and the freedom to choose one's own government and laws.

I have no doubt that we will ultimately prevail in this struggle because our purpose is right and our goal just. There is much that is at stake in this conflict: lives, reputation, trust and the future of this nation and people. This conflict has seen the heaviest fighting since Vietnam and the toll on our forces and their families has been high.

Many have said that with great power comes great responsibility; in fact our own Declaration of Independence says:

> *"But when a long train of abuses and usurpations, pursuing invariably the same Object evinces a design to reduce them under absolute Despotism, it is their right, it is their duty, to throw off such Government, and to provide new Guards for their future security."*

Our own country was founded on the idea of a better life, free from tyranny. As the most powerful nation in the world we have an obligation to assist all people to have the same opportunities we have. Those who stand with us are our friends—those who oppose this right, our enemy.

But is it really as simple as this? Do we really have an obligation as a people to undertake the problems of the world? Are we really justified in helping others to be free from tyranny and oppression?

Look at it from another perspective. God, the One from where all authority on heaven and earth originates, sent His Son into the world to set the captives free and bring hope to the world. In fact, Jesus in his "inauguration speech" in quoting from Isaiah 61 said this:

> *"The Spirit of the Lord is upon Me, Because He has anointed Me To preach the gospel to the poor; He has sent Me to heal the brokenhearted, To proclaim liberty to the captives And recovery of sight to the blind, To set at liberty those who are oppressed; To proclaim the acceptable year of the Lord."*
> —Luke 4:18-19

The very reason Jesus came was to set us free, that the world through him would be saved, to provide a way where there was no way. The very nature of our Lord Jesus Christ is to provide liberty and freedom from sin and oppression. In fact, Jesus said that when He sets you free, you are free indeed.

The Greek word for indeed is "Ontos" which means "truly, in reality, in point of fact, as opposed to what is pretended, fictitious, false, conjectural." In other words He has set us free absolutely and completely. This was the very nature of Jesus. He threw off the bonds of sin and darkness bringing us into His marvelous light.

We have an obligation to bring this good news to those who are in darkness and who suffer without hope. The problem is that many people don't know they are in darkness because the darkness has blinded their eyes to their condition.

Many would say that it is arrogant to suggest that the only way to find hope, peace or fulfillment in life is through Jesus Christ. Maybe it does sound arrogant or close-minded as some suggest, that is until you yourself are set free. Once the scales fall from your eyes you realize that the Way of God and the Love of God are anything but arrogant or forceful.

To those in this land who have new opportunities and a new chance at life for their families, I guarantee they do not view the United States military as oppressive or arrogant; they view it as a liberator and know they have "no better friend." Those who look upon us as arrogant or forceful are those who oppose freedom.

The same is true for those who oppose God and live in rebellion towards Him. To those types of people, anything resembling God or "religion" is a threat to their own identity of darkness, and they strongly appose it. To them, there is "no worse enemy." The scripture gives us an indication of their condition in the first chapter of John's Gospel.

"In Him was life, and the life was the light of men. And the light shines in the darkness, and the darkness did not comprehend it."

—John 1:4-5

"He who believes in Him is not condemned; but he who does not believe is condemned already, because he has not believed in the name of the only begotten Son of God. And this is the condemnation, that the light has come into the world, and men loved darkness rather than light, because their deeds were evil. For everyone practicing evil hates the light and does not come to the light, lest his deeds should be exposed. But he who does the truth comes to the light, that his deeds may be clearly seen, that they have been done in God.

—John 3:18-21

Our goal is to show the people of Iraq the truth of a life that is better, not a life that is American, or western or modern but a life where people are free to make choices for themselves as to how to live. The truth of God's nature is that He is not willing that any should perish but that all would come into everlasting life in Him.

He has set this choice before all of us; it is up to us whether we will accept it or oppose it. Whatever the choice we make, we at least have the freedom to make it.

If you are one who has experienced the beautiful new life and new birth in Christ, you understand this freedom I speak of. Allow God to break your heart for those who have not tasted this for themselves. Pray and ask God to lead you to people who need to experience this truth and gift that God offers.

If you have never experienced this life that Christ offers, make a choice today for freedom. Moses gave a challenge to Israel just before his death as he prepared to hand the leadership of the people over to Joshua:

> *"I call heaven and earth as witnesses today against you, that I have set before you life and death, blessing and cursing; therefore choose life, that both you and your descendants may live."*
> —Deuteronomy 30:19

If you make this choice, the choice of life, you will never be sorry you did. You will emerge on the other side of your prayer to God as the blind man who received his sight after a lifetime in darkness. You will declare to those around you, "I'm not sure what happened to me. All I know is that once I was blind, but now I see!"

From the Battlefield,
Pastor Ryan
Ramadi, Iraq

Application:

There are so many people in our world who do not realize that they are on the wrong team. They have no idea that by not choosing sides they go to the losing team by default. This is a hard reality for many to swallow, but as we who know Christ have come to know, it is, none the less, true. The scripture declares that those who have not believed in the name of the Lord Jesus are condemned. Our responsibility is to share this vital truth in a way that sparks interest and attracts those who are lost to our Jesus. Remember, if bait is not tempting or attractive you would never catch a fish! Pledge today to be that bait that attracts those around you to the One you have in your life.

Prayer:

Beautiful Lord, You have swept me away in Your love and presence. I am daily aware of Your love for me and can't imagine my life without You. Help me Lord to be the fragrance of Jesus and an example that draws people to You. Help me to be a living example of how You lived Your life and to never do or say anything that would bring shame to You. I love You Lord and thank You for first loving me.

In Your Name, Amen.

Day 21

Prevailing Prayer

"The effective, fervent prayer of a righteous man avails much."

—James 5:16

31 December 2004

On this last day of 2004, as I sit here on the battlefield, I am considering all the events of the past year. The ongoing war in Iraq, the devastating school massacre in Russia, the reelection of George W. Bush and of late, the devastating tsunamis in Southwest Asia. So much has happened, and I wonder what direction our world will go in the coming year.

Early this morning as I went out to the walkway around the palace, the sound of the morning prayers filled the air. Each day, five times a day, the mosques in the area broadcast their prayers to Allah to all the people in the area.

Many times these prayers are so loud that I wonder if they don't point the speakers directly at our base! This is a strong reminder for all Muslims to drop what they are doing and pray each day. I see them all the time on their mats next to their trucks and where they work, stop, drop, and pray.

While I certainly do not agree with Islam, this visual and audible reminder is present each day and most Muslims are faithful to pray religiously each day. It made me consider my own prayer life. It also made me think of Daniel, who in the very place I now find myself, served as a faithful example of prayer no matter what the cost.

In the 6th chapter of the Book of Daniel a plot begins to unfold against him because the other leaders under Darius were jealous of him. (Daniel 6:1-6)

The thing that continually sets Daniel apart from others is that he honors God in every aspect of his life and a big part of that was living a life of prayer. Daniel's prayers where not out of obligation or religious practice; they were from the overflow of his heart—a heart completely committed to God. It was his natural expression of love and communion with his Maker.

Daniel distinguished himself *because of the excellent spirit that was in him.* Later we find the schemers devised a plan to destroy Daniel using the very thing that made him stand out:

> *"So these governors and satraps thronged before the king, and said thus to him: "King Darius, live forever! All the governors of the kingdom, the administrators and satraps, the counselors and advisors, have consulted together to establish a royal statute and to make a firm decree, that whoever petitions any god or man for thirty days, except you, O king, shall be cast into the den of lions. Now, O king, establish the decree and sign the writing, so that it cannot be changed, according to the law of the Medes and Persians, which does not alter." Therefore King Darius signed the written decree."*
>
> —Daniel 6:6-9

Notice the empty compliments these men were giving the king. They didn't care a thing about him nor did they care to honor him; they only cared about elevating themselves by destroying Daniel. Will this be the undoing of Daniel? Will he stop praying because of this decree?

"Now when Daniel knew that the writing was signed, he went home. And in his upper room, with his windows open toward Jerusalem, he knelt down on his knees three times that day, and prayed and gave thanks before his God, as was his custom since early days. Then these men assembled and found Daniel praying and making supplication before his God. And they went before the king, and spoke concerning the king's decree: "Have you not signed a decree that every man who petitions any god or man within thirty days, except you, O king, shall be cast into the den of lions?"

—Daniel 6:10-12

When Daniel knew the decree had been signed he did not go and hide himself or cease to live out his faith openly for all to see. He knew that a life without prayer and intimacy with God was a life that was not worth living.

I wonder sometimes how we Christians might react if we had a gun to our head or a knife to our throat as was the case for Daniel. Would we make our stand for Jesus Christ in this type of dire situation? Is prayer that important to you? It says that Daniel *with his windows open* knelt down and prayed as he always did. That is bold!

Is prayer that important to us? Do we truly understand the power of prayer and that it is not a religious obligation, it's a glorious privilege that God has granted us the privilege to commune directly with Him. We all know how the story ends—how Daniel was vindicated by God and rescued from the lion's den.

I wonder what impact this has on our prayer life. Do we live a life that is defined by praying without ceasing? Do we maintain an attitude of "prevailing prayer?" The scripture declares to us: *"The effective, fervent prayer of a righteous man avails much."* (James 5:16b)

Do we have the heart of David, the faithfulness of Daniel and the diligence of Abraham to pray without stopping—to pray for results—to pray always? Can we be found often petitioning the Lord God Almighty for the lost, the sick, and the Nation?

My prayer is that all of us will move past the religious obligation of prayer to the spontaneous outpouring of love, thankfulness and intercession for His Will to be done on earth as it is in heaven.

As I have always around me the reminders of those whose lives are defined by religious prayer, I ask God to take us beyond that to a place of realization that it is a divine privilege and joy as we seek His face in prayer.

From the Battlefield,
Pastor Ryan
Ramadi, Iraq

Application:

I have found in most of my counseling sessions with husbands who are having trouble in their marriages that prayerlessness is a common thread. We limit ourselves so much when we do not maintain a consistent diet of prayer and daily meditation. Prayer is that which unlocks the power of God in a given situation. Prayer is that which directly involves us in the Father's work of building His Kingdom. Rather than spectators, we become participants. God already knows what He will do, but He wants to involve us in this work to grow us and build our faith. Join God in His work and watch your faith muscle grow.

Prayer:

Lord, today I realize that without a consistent and determined prayer life the rest of my walk with You will be ineffective. I ask You today Holy Father to ignite my passion for prayer and refresh my desire to be active with You in seeing Your will done on earth as it is in heaven. I no longer want to pray according to my will Lord, but according to Yours. Create in me a hunger that can only be satisfied on my knees before You.

In the matchless Name of Christ my Lord, Amen.

Day 22

Losing Our Spiritual Sensitivity

"Whoever therefore wants to be a friend of the world makes himself an enemy of God."

—James 4:4

7 January 2005

In this first week of the New Year I have been considering the many blessings that God has for us. In spite of the horrible events in the world these last few months and weeks, God's presence with us is strong. He is intimately acquainted with each of us and with all of the suffering in the world.

Last night as I walked to my room from work I was suddenly aware of something that caused me to go to the Lord in prayer and careful meditation. I was struck with a sudden awareness of my "unawareness!"

On any given day there are the vivid examples of a war that is raging around me—explosions, automatic machine gun fire, jets and helicopters flying overhead, tanks and tracked vehicles moving in the distance, chirping radio chatter and heavily armed personnel guarding the bases. At night you can hear the ominous roar of the Amphibious Assault vehicles as they track to their next raid or assault.

Sometimes the sounds can be heard from many miles away. So many things happening at one time, so many distinct sounds and sights and yet, after being here for awhile, they all begin to fade into the background as a dull and barely noticeable hum.

When I first arrived in Iraq and for several months afterward, every mortar, every rocket that hit close to our base or on our base would immediately wake me out of a deep sleep putting me at once on alert.

Now I find that I sleep right through every event only to find out about it the next night at work. I have found myself on more than one occasion saying, "Wow, I had no idea that we had four mortars hit so close to us!" I just snored right through it.

It reminds me of many people whom I have met and visited who live close to railroad tracks or airports or dairy farms or sewage treatment plants. As soon as you get close you are immediately aware of the loud sound or pungent odor in the air. You find yourself asking them, "How can you stand to live here, how do you sleep?" The response is always the same: "You get used to it after a while."

As I prayerfully considered this state I found myself in, it made me think of my spiritual journey and that of so many others I have met and known over the years. When I was first saved not one sinful thing in the world around me would pass without my noticing it which caused me to cringe in my spirit. The foul language of others around me, the words and actions in movies, the callousness of people to suffering, those things stabbed me sharply in the spirit.

Once born again, I was suddenly aware of all those things as though a curtain had been pulled back from the world revealing its true nature. As the months and years went by I zealously opposed everything that seemed contrary to God and His Word. I had no fear of talking to people about Jesus and laying the truth on the line without apology.

As I continued to mature in my faith it seemed that I became somewhat tolerant of those same things and those same people, somehow justifying my lack of zeal by convincing myself I was becoming more mature and wise in my faith and was choosing my battles more carefully.

It is easy as Christians to find ourselves slipping slowly back into a life that would peacefully co-exist with those around us rather than confront sin. We find that it's easier to look the other way than it is to let someone know his or her language or actions offend us. We would prefer that everyone like us than to confront the issues that Paul speaks of in the first chapter of Romans:

> *"And even as they did not like to retain God in their knowledge, God gave them over to a debased mind, to do those things which are not fitting; being filled with all unrighteousness, sexual immorality, wickedness, covetousness, maliciousness; full of envy, murder, strife, deceit, evil-mindedness; they are whisperers, backbiters, haters of God, violent, proud, boasters, inventors of evil things, disobedient to parents, undiscerning, untrustworthy, unloving, unforgiving, unmerciful; who, knowing the righteous judgment of God, that those who practice such things are deserving of death, not only do the same but also approve of those who practice them."*
> —Romans 1:28-32

Knowing this about the world, about those who do not know God, why is it that we often find ourselves desiring the approval of man? Why is our fear of man more than our fear of God? In our knowledge of God and His Word we know that He has called us to be separate and to be different than those in the world. We are to live *in* the world but not to be *of* the world, or more accurately, to not conform to the world's ideology and values.

Many times we find our sin "senses" dulled because of our insistence on being one of the guys or fitting in rather than standing out. So many times I hear young people or Christians young in their faith saying, "I can go with them; I just won't do the same things they are doing." How long do you think that you can hang out with onions before you begin to smell like an onion too?

Sometimes the sudden reality of my situation hits me hard as I walk in the camp or sit at work. I am in the middle of a raging war in which people are dying nearly every day. There are people a couple hundred yards away from me who would love to kill me. I go about my daily business sometimes without a thought as to the world just on the outside of these walls.

It would only take one insurgent to breach the wall or get past our security to really make for a bad day. I have in a sense become almost oblivious and unaware at times of the true gravity and reality of my situation.

Have we as believers become unaware or oblivious to the true gravity and seriousness of the condition of the world we live in? A world so caught up in sin and darkness, so hopelessly lost that we marvel that God has not yet judged it.

Are we so busy trying to live a peaceful life without standing out that we've become lost in the sea of mediocrity and complacency? We find ourselves "getting used to it" and many times not giving a second thought to sin around us. In the first chapter of Romans Paul had these words to say about the attitude that we as believers are to have about our faith:

> *"For I am not ashamed of the gospel of Christ, for it is the power of God to salvation for everyone who believes, for the Jew first and also for the Greek."*
>
> —Romans 1:16

James also talks about conforming to the world system and the art of "just fitting in" when he says this:

"Adulterers and adulteresses! Do you not know that friendship with the world is enmity with God? Whoever therefore wants to be a friend of the world makes himself an enemy of God. Or do you think that the Scripture says in vain, "The Spirit who dwells in us yearns jealously?"

—James 4:4-5

Essentially, by just trying to fit in, we commit spiritual adultery against our God. We are unfaithful to our Bridegroom when we intermingle with the world system and join ourselves to it. Even the innocence of living peaceably with those around you so as to not offend places us in this uncomfortable position with God.

It is so very important for us to remain vigilant in our opposition to sinful practices and the ways of the world. We must always stand for righteousness and never place our light under a cover. Do not grow weary in well doing nor allow yourself to slide into a state of "spiritual insensitivity" to those worldly forces at work around us.

Stay close to Christ and allow Him to break your heart fresh and new with those things that break His heart. Rise up man and woman of God and step out from among them, for you have been called to be different! You are fearfully and wonderfully made for His good pleasure to carry the torch of the Master into all the world.

From the Battlefield,
Pastor Ryan
Ramadi, Iraq

Application:

After years of fitting in, maybe it's time to stand out a bit! True, it is easier to blend in, fit in, and go with the flow rather than to cause waves. As humans we choose to take the path of least resistance. However, history tends to re-member those who go against the grain, those who let their voices be heard and those who are not satisfied with the status quo. Jesus said to let our light shine before men. Don't allow yourself to become so accustomed to sin and wickedness that you no longer raise a fuss—that you no longer say something when something is wrong. Speak up, man and woman of God.

Prayer:

Lord Jesus, I confess to You today that I have allowed my-self to become numb to the condition of the world around me. I realize today that this is not what You have called me to be. You have called me to be salt and light and to make a difference in a dead and dying world. Please renew my sensitivity to the blaring sound of the war around me. Make me keenly aware that there is a battle going on for each and every soul. Make me more effective and bolder in my witness for You Lord.

In Your Name I pray, Amen.

Day 23

More Than Conquerors

"Yet in all these things we are more than conquerors through Him who loved us."
—Romans 8:37

14 January 2005

God's perspective of our lives, and the situations we encounter daily, is very much like a person who is in a hot air balloon as it hovers over a large parade. From the vantage point of the lofty position in the balloon, one can see the beginning and the end of the parade as well as each float and person on the ground. That person would be able to enter any point in that parade by coming down in the balloon and landing.

He is not subject to the constraints of the parade itself. From our perspective on the ground, all we see is the action that is in front of us as we stand on the street. We are able to see and observe only those floats passing by us.

God is very much like this example in His ability to see all things, past, present and future. He knows what has happened, what is happening and what will happen. We as bystanders have a limited view of these things. We know what has already happened to a certain extent, and we are aware of what is happening now; but with regard to what will happen in the future we are left with only guesses or speculations.

God has told us in advance what will happen to the heavens and the earth. As time passes we get more and more details and understanding of what His Word promises. We see things happening in our world around us and realize that most of it has been predicted in the scriptures. Knowing that God is not subject to time or space the way that we are gives us a better understanding of how He is able to accomplish His work.

On the battlefield I have experienced this phenomenon in a very limited way. In my position as the Patient Evacuation Coordinator I work in the Headquarters of the 1st Marine Division. From this vantage point I have the view of the entire battlefield and the knowledge of most details of operations before and during the event.

I also have come to know all the areas of our operational area and have come to, in some degree, be able to predict the times and places that attacks on our forces will occur. The insurgents have certain areas and times when they like to hit us. What this does for me is to give me a little perspective on what to expect as well as the ability to be prepared ahead of time for casualties.

In some ways this is similar to the overview God has of our lives. He knows the trouble areas where we will be susceptible to attack by the enemy. He knows in advance what will happen. He is able to enter into a situation and protect us many times without our even knowing it.

While I am able to somewhat predict when and where bad things will happen, I am powerless to do anything about it, much less prevent it from happening at all.

So what is one to do with this knowledge? We know that in this world we will have trouble and tribulation, but as Jesus further said to His disciples, *"Be of good cheer, for I have overcome the world."* (John 16:33) We don't always know what will happen in our lives, but we do know the One Who does. He is able to protect and sustain us through all the trials and challenges we could ever face.

I am reminded of the great roll call of the faithful in the 11th chapter of Hebrews where there are two kinds of faithful people listed. There are those who were over-comers and those who persevered in the midst of trials, faithful regardless of the outcome.

In any given situation in our life, God can deliver us and give us great victory or He can divinely strengthen us to persevere through trials, even to the point of death. This gives me great courage and confidence in my God knowing that no matter the outcome, He is able to do exceedingly more than I could ever imagine or hope for.

"And what more shall I say? For the time would fail me to tell of Gideon and Barak and Samson and Jephthah, also of David and Samuel and the prophets: who through faith subdued kingdoms, worked righteousness, obtained promises, stopped the mouths of lions, quenched the violence of fire, escaped the edge of the sword, out of weakness were made strong, became valiant in battle, turned to flight the armies of the aliens. Women received their dead raised to life again. Others were tortured, not accepting deliverance, that they might obtain a better resurrection. Still others had trial of mockings and scourgings, yes, and of chains and imprisonment. They were stoned, they were sawn in two, were tempted, were slain with the sword. They wandered about in sheepskins and goatskins, being destitute, afflicted, tormented—of whom the world was not worthy. They wandered in deserts and mountains, in dens and caves of the earth. And all these, having obtained a good testimony through faith, did not receive the promise, God having provided something better for us, that they should not be made perfect apart from us."

—Hebrews 11:32-40

So whether our final outcome in a given situation is good or not so good in our perspective, God is always with us. He promises us that He will never leave us nor forsake us. In our limited perspective and view, we always assume this means we will be granted a great victory. We are quick to pull out such verses as Romans 8:28 or 8:37.

"And we know that all things work together for good to those who love God, to those who are the called according to His purpose."

"Yet in all these things we are more than conquerors through Him who loved us."

While these verses are certainly true and promises we can stand on, "good" and "more than conquerors" does not always mean what we think. Good is relative to only one thing, God's Will. For there is no good apart from God's perfect Will. We are quick to see these verses in light of the wonderful deliverance of Meshach, Shadrach, and Abed-Nego, but slow to remember it in light of Stephen!

While the three companions of Daniel had one "like the Son of God" in the furnace with them, Stephen had a "standing ovation" from the Son of God. Which one was more than a conqueror? Which had all things work together for their good? The answer is both.

The great thing about each of those named in Hebrews 11 is that they all were over-comers in that they endured in their faith no matter the outcome. Their version of "all things work together for good" was in the accomplishing of God's Will to the end.

Jesus' perspective of "more than a conqueror" was total and complete obedience to the Will of His Father in heaven. In this, He was more than a conqueror having conquered death and the grave. He now sits at the right hand of the Father ever making intercession for us.

You can rest in the certain knowledge that God knows the beginning and the end and is always by our side. Be of good courage and faith in every situation regardless of the outcome, knowing that the testing of your faith produces in you a Godly character and strength that will enable you to stand for God no matter what.

So, with my view from the battlefield, no matter what the outcome of the battle, I stand in faith for each person. I pray that in all circumstances God will be glorified and the Kingdom furthered—whether that means miraculous deliverance from harm or the faith to endure through the worst of what the enemy deals us. God is always faithful. God is always on the Throne.

From the Battlefield,
Pastor Ryan
Ramadi, Iraq

Application:

How can a loving God let bad things happen? Why do bad things happen to good people? We've all heard these questions and wondered what the answer could be. Too many people look at circumstances as the determining factor for whether something is good or bad. This is not, however, God's measuring stick. His Will being done in His timing is His perfect measuring stick. Nothing else goes into this equation. This does not mean that God is not loving and compassionate; it simply gives His compassion and mercy a stage upon which to operate. No matter what the outcome of your situation, trust God and know His Will is perfect, even when we don't understand.

Prayer:

Lord, today I choose to trust You no matter what the wind and the waves may do. I know that Your will is not determined by circumstances or how I think something should turn out. Your Will shall be accomplished regardless of those factors. I trust You for every detail of my life and surrender my fears and anxieties to Your perfect plan and love for me. Help me to let go completely and know that all things are working together for my good because You have called me according to Your purposes.

In Your Holy Name, Amen.

Day 24

Prepare to Stand, Stand Strong!

"Therefore take up the whole armor of God, that you may be able to withstand in the evil day, and having done all, to stand."

—Ephesians 6:13

21 January 2005

Today as I write I am fresh off an experience that has left a solid mark on my spirit. Two days ago we went through a base-wide drill to help prepare us for an attack by insurgents on our base. This is something we do often during our time here. At a set time the "big voice" went off (this is the speaker system that is up all over the base that sounds the alarm when we are attacked), and all of us went to our appointed place of duty.

There are many things that must take place when the big voice goes off. All Marines, Soldiers, Sailors and other personnel on the base know exactly what they are supposed to do when this happens. This knowledge has come from training and class after class to deeply ingrain this plan into our brains.

Some Marines and Soldiers have set battle stations that they have to report to immediately. These are defensive positions around the perimeter of the base, important places on the base. Others, such as medical personnel, have appointed places to be in order to react to any casualties that may result from the attack.

Chaplains are to make their way as quickly as possible to the medical aid station to be on hand to pray and comfort any wounded personnel that may come in. Others man communication and monitoring stations. Those who don't specifically have a defensive position are to report to the nearest hardened structure or building for cover and call in to the command post for full accountability.

The point to this is that every person on the base knows exactly where and what they are to be doing in the event of an attack. Each warrior is also to have all his or her protective war gear on—helmet, flak vest, first aid kit and weapon.

So, when two days ago we had one of these drills, everyone was in their appointed place of duty and knew exactly what to do. This creates an amazing feeling of confidence and security for everyone.

Yesterday, fresh off this successful drill, the base did in fact come under heavy attack from the enemy. About mid-day, as most were coming to and from the mess hall, the enemy launched a fierce attack that lasted close to ten minutes.

There were mortars and rockets going over us with their distinct whistling sound and all too familiar heavy thuds as they hit on and near the base. Some fell short into the Euphrates River next to us, and some hit various places of the base and the base across the river.

Immediately everyone took up defensive positions around the base. Within minutes everyone was where he or she needed to be and the base was secured. We weathered the attack and not one person was killed or wounded. This is absolutely amazing when you consider that nearly 20 rockets and mortars were incoming. It was one of the biggest attacks we have had since I've been here.

The constant training and educating of our people made the difference. Of course, I have another reason why I believe we were protected—all the faithful prayers from back home.

This brought to the forefront of my mind the similar spiritual battle that all of us as followers of Jesus Christ go through on a daily basis. As leaders in the Body of Christ, pastors, teachers, and other leaders have the great responsibility to train up Christians in the ways of God and ground them in His Word. We must train them in the ways of Godliness and prayer, developing them to be mature and strong followers of Christ.

As individual believers we have the personal responsibility to listen to our leaders and learn what God has for us in our life with Him. We must take the personal initiative to draw close to God and to grow in our faith each day.

When the Body of Christ is functioning in unity and the way God has directed in the scriptures, we too will be ready for the attacks of the enemy when they come. Each member of the Body of Christ will be where he or she is supposed to be—carrying out the function within the church that God has called them to do. Paul writes to the Corinthian Church about this subject:

> *"For as the body is one and has many members, but all the members of that one body, being many, are one body, so also is Christ. For by one Spirit we were all baptized into one body—whether Jews or Greeks, whether slaves or free—and have all been made to drink into one Spirit. For in fact the body is not one member but many."*
>
> —1 Corinthians 12:20-26

Each member working in unity, together as a team in the strength and power of the Holy Spirit, is able to repel the lies, deception, and fiery darts of the wicked one. As we on Camp Blue Diamond know that we are to have on our full armor that the military has given us, so too, must we as believers have on our full God given armor and be ready to wield the *most* powerful weapon, the Word of God.

For us in the combat zone, having this protective gear on or with us at all times is second nature to us, just like breathing or eating. We all know how important this protection is in the event of attack. God has declared the same thing to us as believers. We must work in unity, each knowing our part and place in the body of Christ, and each putting on the whole armor of God.

> *"Finally, my brethren, be strong in the Lord and in the power of His might. Put on the whole armor of God, that you may be able to stand against the wiles of the devil. For we do not wrestle against flesh and blood, but against principalities, against powers, against the rulers of the darkness of this age, against spiritual hosts of wickedness in the heavenly places. Therefore take up the whole armor of God, that you may be able to withstand in the evil day, and having done all, to stand. Stand therefore, having girded your waist with truth, having put on the breastplate of righteousness, and having shod your feet with the preparation of the gospel of peace; above all, taking the shield of faith with which you will be able to quench all the fiery darts of the wicked one. And take the helmet of salvation, and the sword of the Spirit, which is the Word of God; praying always with all prayer and supplication in the Spirit, being watchful to this end with all perseverance and supplication for all the saints..."*
>
> —Ephesians 6:10-18

Paul knew as he wrote to the Ephesian church that it was not a matter of if the enemy would attack, it was when. They needed to stand together in unity and prepare for the inevitable. Train, train, train! Be grounded in the faith and ready at anytime for the principalities, powers and darkness that will come.

Just as we here in Iraq must be prepared for anything, we as believers must not fail to be ready to stand strong in the day of trouble. May God bless you richly this week.

Pastor Ryan
Ramadi, Iraq

Application:

Most of us have heard the wise old saying "You've got to stand for something or you fall for anything." For us as believers this "something" is the truth of God's Word. If we do not know the Word well, we will not be able to identify counterfeits when confronted with them. In essence, we must train, train, train in the Word of God and know our place in Christ. Remember, an enemy is looking for the weak spot, not the reinforced strong point. Don't let the enemy find a weak spot in your wall.

Prayer:

Heavenly Father, I pray a prayer of faith today knowing that when I ask anything according to Your will it will be done. My petition is for my heart and life to be fortified and secure, well grounded and strong in the knowledge of Your ways. Give me wisdom beyond my years to rightly divide and apply Your living Words not only to my own life but also to those around me in need. Fill me with Your Holy Spirit and with power to be an overcomer and more than a conqueror in You.

In Your precious and Holy Name, Amen.

Day 25

Hold Me in Your Arms Lord

"During your times of trial and suffering, when you
see only one set of footprints, it was then that I carried you."

from "Footprints in the Sand"
by Mary Stevenson

28 January 2005

There have been many difficult situations I have seen
and dealt with during my six months here in Iraq. There are
the trials of being away from my family and church, the
extended hours and days of continuous operations, the hor-
rors of death and suffering, and the reality of situations that
are out of my control. With all these hardships, none has
compared to the circumstances of this past week.

The Book of Acts recounts that throughout the first
missionary journey of Paul and Barnabas they encountered
great opposition and trials in the midst of great response to
the message of Christ they preached. After a great success
in Iconium, an angry mob was stirred up against the two
evangelists, and they were forced to flee to Lystra.

They continued to proclaim the wonderful news of Jesus Christ, and it was at this place that an amazing encounter took place. Listening intently to Paul's preaching was a
man who had been a cripple from birth. This man had never
walked and had no strength in his feet:

*"And in Lystra a certain man without strength in his
feet was sitting, a cripple from his mother's womb,
who had never walked. This man heard Paul speaking. Paul, observing him intently and seeing that he
had faith to be healed, said with a loud voice, "Stand
up straight on your feet!" And he leaped and walked."*
—Acts 14:8-10

If the story had ended with this great victory, what an
amazing thing it would be! However, the results of this
great miracle were less than pleasant for Paul:

*"Then Jews from Antioch and Iconium came there;
and having persuaded the multitudes, they stoned
Paul and dragged him out of the city, supposing him
to be dead."*
—Acts 14:19

We recall from the ministry of Jesus the story of a
man who was born blind. Jesus' healing of this man shows
His disciples His power over what seems to be a hopeless
situation. We recall the unconventional method that Jesus
uses in this healing process of using spit and mud. The re-
sulting testimony of the healed man when questioned by
those in authority is unforgettable. His words ring out in
our hearts:

*"So they again called the man who was blind, and
said to him, "Give God the glory! We know that this
Man is a sinner." He answered and said, "Whether
He is a sinner or not I do not know. One thing I know:
that though I was blind, now I see."*
—John 9:24-25

The most amazing thing in this man's life had just
taken place. He had never known what it was like to see the

light of day. In fact, the situation was so amazing and wonderful to him that he knew little else than the fact that only moments ago his world consisted of darkness, and now he saw clearly the world around him.

The story does not end here. After the greatest victory in his life came a great trial. He was reviled and excommunicated because the miracle did not fit into the Pharisee's box. With great victory, comes great trial.

After the amazing things that God has done, when we later come into trial it would be easy for us to get discouraged. Blame, complaint, and self-pity destroy Christian experience. The toughness of the circumstances creates new "stretch" in our experience.

Our new capacity must be filled with the Holy Spirit Who brings joy. Grumbling and downhearted Christians never show the world that Jesus is risen! The deeper the submarine goes the greater must be its resistance to pressure. God's Spirit pressurizes the chambers or our inner man.

I have mentioned all of this above to lead into this week's story. For the last two weeks we have enjoyed wonderful victory in our Bible studies on Sundays. Two weeks ago following a study in the first chapter of Galatians and specifically the story of the bondservant, a young man stepped forward to receive Jesus as his Lord and Savior!

We had been praying for him for weeks and to see it happen brought joy to all of us. Last week following the Bible study we began to pray. There were 10 of us there and one by one each person prayed.

By the time the second person began praying, pouring her heart out before God, the Holy Spirit fell upon all of us. The sweet presence of Jesus was with us and the praying went on for some time. Each of us experienced newness in our spirits and strength for the coming week. Every one of us knew that God had walked among us during that time and were humbled and filled with great joy.

Coming off these last two weeks of victory and joy in Christ we then entered into this week. I had no idea what was in store for us. No one could have guessed or predicted what would occur on the battlefield.

Tuesday morning I was on duty at 0145 when a call came in that we had a downed helicopter. This has happened a few times since we have been here so we all knew what to do. I immediately notified all the surrounding medical facilities to prepare for a possible mass casualty situation. A ground force was immediately dispatched to provide security around the crash site.

I began to pray for those involved, hoping that it was not as bad as it seemed to be. Later we began getting details in as to what kind of aircraft and the number of people on board. It was a CH-53 helicopter, which is the largest in our fleet.

Then word came in that it was fully loaded with 27 passengers and four crew members. Our hearts sank. I still continued to pray holding on to hope that it was not as bad as it looked. The initial report came in from the ground team. 18 confirmed dead. My heart hurt so bad I could barely hold it in. A little while later the word from the ground came in: There were no survivors.

The heaviness that spread throughout the command operations center was beyond description. By now the Commanding General had been awakened and was in the command center. The look on his face told the whole story. He was devastated. I began to think of all the families back home. So many lives would be changed and affected forever.

I wanted to leave and go be alone somewhere. I went outside to sit under the stars and pray. I had been sitting for several minutes when one of the crew members from the desk next to mine came running out to me. She said, "We have four urgent surgical patients!"

I ran back inside and sat down. Another incident had occurred. A coordinated ambush had happened, and we had two more that were killed and seven wounded, four of them badly. By the end of the night two more of these died despite my greatest efforts to get them to the right place. They just didn't make it. They had severe head wounds and I would find out later that they would not have lived even with the greatest doctors in the world.

At this particular time of the morning all I knew is that we had just lost 35 Marines and one Sailor. My heart and mind were numb. I couldn't think or even move.

At the same time I got an email from home that there were some bad things happening there as well. A good friend had just found out that his grandmother had cancer. My niece was having complications with her pregnancy. My son was having a hard time in school.

When my relief came in I put on my protective vest and helmet and slowly walked home to my room. I sat on the end of my bed for over an hour. I had taken all I could take, and I was emotionally shutting down.

I laid my head down and closed my eyes. I tried to pray but only saw the images of the night in my head, the images of families who would soon receive a knock on their door that would forever alter their lives. I prayed, I cried bitterly, and I finally fell asleep. My sleep was filled with dreams and images of what had happened. All I could do was cry out to God,

"Please help me to get through this. Please help the Marines and their families to get through this."

The next night came word that my niece had delivered a stillborn little boy. She and her husband were devastated. I was heartbroken. I was able to call and talk to both of them briefly and pray with them. We all found comfort in this.

Tonight I look over the events of the past few days and I wonder how I could endure any more. I wonder what purpose this has all served. I think of my wife and the immense pressure and stress she is under this week and while I've been gone.

"What is it all for Lord? Can You bring something good out of this? Can you mend all the broken hearts?"

As I look back over the ministry of Paul, Barnabas, and Jesus I am assured in my spirit that the answer is YES! The sun will rise tomorrow, and the Lord's mercies are new each day. Though I have walked through the literal valley of the shadow of death this week I will come to the mountain. I have taken great comfort and strength in looking down into the sand and finding just one set of footprints. "Thank You Lord for carrying me in Your arms this week."

Pastor Ryan
Ramadi, Iraq

Application:

When we find ourselves in the midst of great pressure and circumstances that seem to be too much for us we can be sure of one thing—God will never leave nor forsake us. His Word promises this, but too often we find it easy to be swept away by the gravity and magnitude of the situation rather than the power and glory of God who is in control of the situation. It is our human nature and weakness that limits our ability to trust God fully in each situation. The challenge is to allow the lesson to increase our faith and to be better prepared for the next trial.

Prayer:

Lord, today I choose to lay my fears, insecurities, and lack of faith at Your feet and trust You completely. In more times than I can count I have depended upon myself to get through hard times and to process the difficult things I go through. Help me to take on the likeness of Jesus Christ and look through the lens He provided for me through His perfect life on earth. Give me eyes to see and vision beyond vision for the things of Your heavenly Kingdom. Help me to endure and persevere in all things.

In Jesus' Name, Amen.

Day 26

A Greater Weight of Glory

"For momentary, light affliction is producing for us an eternal weight of glory far beyond all comparison..."

—2 Corinthians 4:17

4 February 2005

This week has seen many changes on the battlefield for me, personally. This was my last week at Camp Blue Diamond in Ramadi, and all the Patient Evacuation duties were turned over to the new team. There is almost a bittersweet feeling about turning this job over to a new crew—bitter in that you come to know all the people you work with and all the people in the medical facilities throughout the operational area.

You build a camaraderie and respect for one another. You rejoice together when things go well, and you mourn together when things go badly. After six months you become close to many of them. The "sweet" part comes in the fact that I am now that much closer to coming home to my wife, family and church. I feel the anticipation building in me even as I write this.

All this to say, I felt like my time was winding down and that I would really not experience anything too significant during my last few weeks here. I'm at a new base waiting to come home, out of a job with lots of time on my hands. It has given me an opportunity to get some much needed rest and to unwind from the very emotionally charged job of moving all our wounded servicemen and women.

This however was to be short lived. One of the most profound and emotional events was to jar me back to reality.

Several nights ago, my first night here at Camp Al Taqaddum, I had an opportunity to go to one of the medical facilities that I frequently sent patients to during my tenure as the evacuation coordinator. I thanked them and was able to spend some time seeing how things worked on the other end of the phone.

While I was talking with the team, the call came notifying them of incoming wounded. I was interested to watch and see how the whole process worked on this end, so the team invited me to stick around. Fifteen minutes later the chopper arrived, and the patient was hurried to the operating room for emergency surgery. There was a real sense of urgency in all the doctors, nurses and corpsmen. I soon found out why.

The patient had been 15 meters away when a rocket hit, and he was badly wounded by shrapnel. When he arrived off the helo, he was not breathing, and they were bag ventilating him. The team worked quickly to save his life, doing everything humanly possible to revive him and stop the bleeding. I was observing on the side of the operating room, and I began to pray for this young man.

Then came the news that made my heart skip a beat. The young man was from Camp Blue Diamond and worked in the same operations center that I had just left. Chances were I knew him well. When I found out his name, I realized I did know him. He worked a few chairs over from me. I saw him every day, and most of my crew knew him.

The doctors continued franticly to work, doing all they could. Despite their best efforts, he passed away before my eyes. I felt like I couldn't breathe, like I was waiting to exhale.

I was in shock in my heart. Here was a guy I had worked with everyday. We had not lost anyone who worked closely with us the whole time I was doing my job. I also realized a while later that he was the husband of a nurse whom I had worked with in the Emergency Room last year.

This was a strangely personal experience that hurt badly in my heart. I knew she would be devastated. I found myself praying for her all night long and through the remainder of this week.

The next day the rest of my crew from the Direct Air Support Center arrived. They were delayed one day in coming. Several of those who arrived had been in my Bible studies while we were all at Blue Diamond. When I realized that they had been very close to where the rocket had hit the night before, I was again anxious in my spirit. For some reason I knew there was more to this already heartbreaking story.

My suspicions were confirmed. That morning there came a knock at my door. When I opened the door there stood five members of my team with strange looks on their faces. Three of them had been in my Bible study, and the other two I had worked closely with.

I immediately knew something was up. I invited them in to sit down and share what was on their hearts. It turns out that all of them were in the command center when the rocket hit. This time the impact was closer than it had ever been while we were there. After the impact the Gunnery Sergeant ran outside to see if anyone was hit. That's when she found the Captain. She was the first to reach him and immediately began treating him.

He was in bad shape and shaking as she held his head in her arms and one of his hands. Another Marine arrived and began to apply bandages to try to stop the bleeding.

She continued to talk with the Captain trying to keep him awake.

She was crying now as she told me this story and the experience had changed her forever. She continued to hold his hand and talk to him. He told her that he couldn't see anything, and she continued telling him to look at her.

"Look at me, look at me. You're going to be ok. We're going to get you out of here."

She continued to hold him until the chopper arrived and whisked him away to the medical facility where I was. I knew nothing of what had happened on the other end of the helicopter ride—I knew now.

As she finished telling me her story with tears streaming down her face, I was at a loss for words. My heart was crushed, and I felt so badly for her having experienced something so horrible. Not knowing what to say I gathered them all together, and we began to pray.

I prayed and prayed for God's peace and love to surround her and each of them. I prayed that God would help all of us to process what had happened and to give us even more compassion for people, knowing that we never know when our time is up. I also prayed that He would give us an added measure of urgency in sharing Jesus with others.

When we finished, God gave me the right words for her. I told her that she was one of the last people the Captain had seen before he slipped into unconsciousness. Jesus used her to talk to him and comfort him with His love.

Though it was hard to understand at the time, God in His love and mercy had sent her, a woman filled with God's Holy Spirit and love, to show love and compassion to this man before he died. The last thing he experienced on this earth was the love of God through one of His servants.

I told her it was not by accident that she was there. It may be hard to deal with at first, but God will use this experience to give her greater compassion and love for all people. Yes, this was by God's design. Tears continued to flow down her face, and I was weeping now as well. I gathered them all together and hugged them. None of us would ever be the same after this. It reminded me of a scripture:

> *"Therefore we do not lose heart, but though our outer man is decaying, yet our inner man is being renewed day by day. For momentary, light affliction is producing for us an eternal weight of glory far beyond all comparison, while we look not at the things which are seen, but at the things which are not seen; for the things which are seen are temporal, but the things which are not seen are eternal."*
>
> —2 Corinthians 4:16-18

During the last six months I have been through more and seen more than most people will see in a lifetime. God has allowed me to go through the most difficult time in my life, but through it I have been refined and conformed more into the image of His Son Jesus. As a hunk of clay on a potter's wheel, He has performed painful surgery on me and created a man of prayer that did not exist before.

I now know what it means to pray without ceasing. This deployment has been one long prayer session. I can't help but wonder what God has planned for me in the months to come. I can't help but wonder what kind of a vessel he has crafted me into, what will be my purpose.

I know this for sure, my light affliction is but for a moment, and it is working for me a far more exceedingly and eternal weight of glory. May you realize this week that each fire, each trial will enable you more to give to a lost and dying world.

From the Battlefield,
Pastor Ryan
Al Taqaddum, Iraq

Application:

We have all heard the saying "I can't see the forest for the trees." As this saying suggests, often we can't see the bigger picture or plan that God has when we are the midst of difficulty, pain, or irritation. I remember being in a restaurant in my hometown where they still allowed smoking inside. My eyes had been bothering me for a few days prior because of allergies and dryness. I was very irritated with this man sitting behind us who seemed to light one cigarette after another while we were trying to eat. My eyes burned and I thought about getting huffy with him regarding his lack of respect for us. I bit my tongue for some reason and chose to just leave with my family. My grandfather came out of the restaurant after I did and told me the man had pulled him aside as he was leaving and told him it was refreshing to see a Christian family praying and eating together in a place that usually only served railroad workers, bikers and cowboys. I had almost blown my witness because I was irritated. Look at each trial as an opportunity rather than a problem and see what God will do.

Prayer:

Lord, sometimes I feel that I have to demand my rights and let people know when they have done me wrong. I sometimes feel like, "How dare they use that kind of language or act that way around me!" Lord, forgive me for my arrogance and help me to see Your divine purpose for me no matter where I may find myself. Help me to be sensitive to Your Holy Spirit so that I may draw people to Your Son Jesus. Thank you for every opportunity You give me Lord to tell people about You; whether that be with words, or actions.

In Your Holy Name I pray, Amen.

Day 27

The Other Side

"Then Elijah said to him, "Stay here, please, for the LORD has sent me on to the Jordan." But he said, "As the LORD lives, and as your soul lives, I will not leave you!"
—2 Kings 2:6

11 February 2005

As I am nearing the end of my time in Iraq, reflecting on my experience has revealed something interesting that again parallels our life in Christ. When I thought about all I had been through during my time here and those experiences of others around me, I discovered a common thread.

Whether it was an individual operation, a full mission, a specific time period, or the deployment as a whole, I have found that most of us get through with a very specific mentality. This mentality or attitude is this:

"I just need to get through this mission. After it is done, everything will be fine. We just need to get through with Fallujah, and then everything will work out. We just need to get past the elections, and then the country will stabilize. I just need to get through this deployment and get home to my family. Then everything will be OK."

I am reminded of the heartbreaking story I read this week of a 19-year-old Marine named Jason Redifer who was only one week away from coming home when he was killed in action here in Iraq.

His mother had been anticipating his return and was already feeling the excitement of the reunion. The account she gave in the interview of how she felt that moment when the two Marines in dress blues came up to her tore my heart out.

I think more than anything it was because several weeks ago, following the helicopter crash which took the lives of 31 of our Marines and a Sailor, I had dreams all night long that continued to wake me up. They were not dreams of those who had perished; they were dreams of the "knock" at the door and the horrible moment when a mother, father, wife or husband would be told the worst possible news.

I had horrible dreams and even for the next few days as I prayed for these families. I would have this sickening feeling in my stomach knowing that so many families around the United States were getting that very news. Now, reading about Jason's mother Rhonda Winfield recount this experience first hand has opened many of those wounds in my spirit.

I can't help but think to myself that I know he was saying, "I just need to get through to the other side of this mission; then I am home free."

I have heard countless others say this same thing. It is the kind of statement that breaches the lips of nearly every United States military person in this conflict. We know that the job we are doing is noble, just, and important. We know that the effect it has had on the Iraqi people is something vital that they will never forget.

Seeing children playing and people walking about with smiles on their faces and hope in their steps confirms this in all of us. That does not change the fact that we all want to get the job done, and get home. I just want to get to the "other side" of this deployment.

Thinking of all these things and reflecting as I have this week brought to my mind some examples from the scriptures of those who had the "other side" in sight.

One such example was that of Elijah and his young apprentice Elisha. In the last moments of the prophet Elijah's life on earth, he traveled to several places, finally ending up at the Jordan River. Each time he bade his young protégé to remain while he went on further.

Each time Elisha refused, wanting to spend every moment possible with his master before he was taken into heaven. He craved every possible morsel of spiritual sustenance he could gather from his master. He was not content to remain behind; he wanted more.

"Then Elijah said to him, "Stay here, please, for the LORD has sent me on to the Jordan." But he said, "As the LORD lives, and as your soul lives, I will not leave you!" So the two of them went on. And fifty men of the sons of the prophets went and stood facing them at a distance, while the two of them stood by the Jordan. Now Elijah took his mantle, rolled it up, and struck the water; and it was divided this way and that, so that the two of them crossed over on dry ground. And so it was, when they had crossed over, that Elijah said to Elisha, "Ask! What may I do for you, before I am taken away from you?" Elisha said, "Please let a double portion of your spirit be upon me."

—2 Kings 2:6-9

There are several things about this passage that are striking. The first is Elisha's strong determination to continue to be in the company of the man of God. He so longed to glean knowledge and substance from the rich spiritual arsenal of this great man.

The other thing I noticed is the company of 50 men of the sons of the prophets who watched from a distance as Elijah and Elisha crossed over the Jordan. These were not novices in the faith. They were prophetic students who had detailed knowledge of the scriptures and the life of faith.

However, even knowing from their previous prophetic declarations that Elijah would be taken from them that day, they were content to stay on the safe side of the river. Elisha would have nothing to do with this and knew that he had to go to the "other side" with his master. The result was the bestowal of a double portion of Elijah's spirit upon him. Wow! What perseverance and persistence he had to see more and experience more of what God had for his life.

Another such example was that of the multitudes who listened to Jesus preach on the hills around the Sea of Galilee. During one such episode news came to Jesus of the death of John the Baptist. The news weighed heavily on Him, and He withdrew to a solitary place. The multitudes of people heard where He was and set out on foot to find Him even though he was far off from any of the villages and the towns.

There were no 7-Elevens or restaurants along the way for them to eat yet they pressed on to the "other side" of the lake. The only thing they knew was that Jesus was there, and they had to get to Him. What followed was the miraculous feeding of the 5,000. In our pursuit of God, we too must be ready to brave the unknown factors of the other side to be with our Lord.

Jesus came to this earth for a specific purpose. He came to bring God's message of love and to provide the method for entering into eternal life. Most of His ministry could be categorized as "walking through the valley of the shadow of death." There were more down times than up.

Most places He went there were many more opposed to His message than those who believed. Still, He resolutely set His eyes on the "other side." You might say,

"Other side of what?" The other side of the Cross of Calvary. Everything He did on earth was dramatically propelling Him to the pain and anguish of the Cross. His ministry and life pointed to a six hour climax on a hill outside Jerusalem reserved for criminals and thieves.

Jesus knew if He could just get beyond the Cross, if He could just get to the "other side" the glory of the resurrection awaited Him. Although He trudged through that dark valley, He came to the highest mountain top conquering death and the grave.

We must have a prevailing passion in life to go beyond our present circumstances, to go further than we believe possible to bring glory to God in our lives. We must take on the attitude of the woman in the crowd with the issue of blood. She pressed through to the "other side" of the crowd, knowing that all she needed to do was touch His garment for her healing. Or perhaps we need the determination of Jacob who wrestled with God and would not let go until He blessed him. The experience transformed him from Jacob the deceiver to Israel, father of the 12 tribes. We strive to press on through any barrier, any obstacle knowing that God is Who He says He is and that He rewards those who diligently seek Him.

Have you found yourself lately going through a time when you wonder how or if you will make it through? Have your personal circumstances become so difficult and trying that you have lost your will to continue? Know this, on the other side Jesus is waiting. He has promised rest to the weary and the removal of burdens from those who bear them. Press on brothers and sisters, press on to the "other side."

From the Battlefield,
Pastor Ryan
Taqaddum, Iraq

Application:

There can be no doubt that we often find ourselves in situations that are less than fun. There are times that we begin to question God's wisdom or wonder if He really sees what we are going through. These are the times when we should have great anticipation that something wonderful is coming. These are the times when we need to take on a prevailing, persistent, and persevering attitude. Remember, God's Will is in no way determined by our opinion. Rather, our opinion and feelings should be determined by conforming to the perfect Will of God.

Prayer:

Gracious Lord, Father of Lights and all creation, send Your loving Spirit and presence to comfort and surround all who read this. May Your Holy Spirit give them the assurance of Your enduring love for them through any and all situations in life that they may encounter. We are confident at this moment that You have all matters within Your control and grasp and trust You for Your perfect will to be done.

In the Name of Jesus we pray, Amen.

Day 28

The Homecoming

"But sanctify the Lord God in your hearts, and always be ready to give a defense to everyone who asks you a reason for the hope that is in you, with meekness and fear…"

—1 Peter 3:15

18 February 2005

This week as I meditate on God's Word and think about my homecoming that draws very near, I can't help but wonder what it is that makes me so excited about coming home.

There is the quick draw answer; I will be with my wife and family again.

There is the secondary answer; I will be with my church family and friends again.

Then there is another more selfish, yet very important reason—I will be able to have a venti at Starbucks and a slice of pepperoni pizza!

Seriously though, what is it about coming home that keeps me awake at night? Why are my thoughts nearly consumed with this quickly approaching date? What is it about leaving this country where so many good things and bad things have happened? As I think about this I consider the scripture that the Holy Spirit inspired Peter to write:

"But sanctify the Lord God in your hearts, and always be ready to give a defense to everyone who asks you a reason for the hope that is in you, with meekness and fear..."

—1 Peter 3:15

This is an amazing passage which gives us the motivation to be prepared at anytime to defend the Gospel and share our faith with others. But, when you look closer you find what it is exactly that we are to share with others—the HOPE that is within us. The Greek word for hope in this verse is *eplis* which means "the expectation of good, the joyful and confident expectation of eternal life; the author of hope or He who is its foundation."

What is the hope that we have? First, we have the expectation of good things to come, both in this life and the next. Second, we have the confidence in our eternal place in heaven. And last, we have hope in the One who alone is worthy of our hope. The One who is the object, author, and finisher of our faith.

Plainly said, our hope is that we will be going home some day to be forever with our Savior and King, the One who gave Himself for us.

When I think of my earthly perspective of what it means to be going home after a long time away, I can't help but also look to my final "homecoming" that is also rapidly approaching. While here on earth I will enjoy the wonder and overwhelming happiness of gathering my wife into my arms again. Soon I will experience the unspeakable and glorious joy of being gathered into my Lord's arms forever!

The hope that we are to share with others is not so much what this life has to offer, but the next one brings. The hope we have would be sadly deficient if it were just about a better life here on earth. If we could not look longingly heavenward to eternity with Christ, we would not have much more to offer those who are searching than another feel good organization or club.

When I think of the day I will see my wife, it is almost too much to bear for my little mind! But when I think ahead to the day that I will enter into His rest and hear those words, "Well done, good and faithful servant," the thought warms my every part and compels me to tell as many people as I possibly can about this hope in me. I think of the words of the song by Mercy Me which say,

> *Surrounded by Your Glory,*
> *What will my heart feel?*
> *Will I dance for you, Jesus?*
> *Or in awe of You, be still?*
> *Will I stand in Your presence,*
> *Or to my knees will I fall?*
> *Will I sing 'Hallelujah!'?*
> *Will I be able to speak at all?*
> *I can only imagine,*
> *I can only imagine!*

When I hear the words of this song I am immediately reminded of the hope that is within me. That hope is nothing short of the fullness of meeting my Jesus face to face. Seeing my precious Kellee again face to face will be amazing, and it is about all I think about right now. But even that can not compare to what it will be like to stand in His presence.

Does your life shout out that your hope is in Jesus? Do you live each day in the hope that you can share that with someone who doesn't know Him? Do you look forward to that day with nothing holding you back? Is there anything on this planet that you look forward to or love more than Jesus Christ, the King of Kings, and the Lord of Lords?

If you can't honestly say that Jesus is the reason and the hope of your life, surrender yourself completely to Him now and never look back. You will NEVER be sorry! At this time next week I should be home with Kellee and Cameron, but in the forefront of my mind I look forward with even more longing to the day I will see Jesus. I pray this is your hope as well.

From the Battlefield,
Pastor Ryan
Taqaddum, Iraq

Application:

Are we living our life for the world and the pleasures and pursuits contained therein, or are we living with an expectation of greater things to come? When we see the signs of the time come to pass in our world are we quick to do as the scriptures declare and "look up for our redemption draws near?" Or do we think, "Lord, please don't come now, I have too many things I still want to do in life." We do not look forward to death and being with Jesus primarily because we still look forward to this life and our own pursuits more. The truth is, everyone looks forward to going to heaven but no one wants to die to get there. Set your eyes on the pearl of great price, rather than on the cheap dime store imitations that this world has to offer.

Prayer:

Lord, help me today to have a Kingdom perspective on life rather than a "Lord, please bless me in what I want to do" perspective. Help me to place You first in all things and to truly have a growing desire inside to be with You with every passing day. Break my heart Lord for those things that break Your heart and give me Your priorities for my life. Please take my heart and mold it into the image and likeness of Christ. Remove my selfish motives and tenden-cies and replace them with a heart that only beats for You.

These things I pray in Jesus' Name, Amen.

Day 29

Something Big Is Coming!

"Where no oxen are, the trough is clean; but much increase comes by the strength of an ox."

—Proverbs 14:4

23 February 2005

A dear pastor friend of mine once said, "The train of adversity usually arrives at the station around the same time as the train of revival." My, how true this is. It seems that whenever something good is happening or about to happen, the enemy works overtime to spoil everything.

I found this to be especially true on the battlefield in Iraq. From the turnover of power from the Coalition Provisional Authority to the Iraqi Government to the January 2005 elections, one thing is sure. The enemy was working extra hard to destroy any victory that the people or military might enjoy.

Although we surprised everyone by turning power over two days before the 30 June 2004, deadline, the insurgency made up for lost time afterward by attacking any and every position they could. Although military casualties were minimal on the January 30th Election Day, civilian casualties were high, especially in and around Baghdad. Their actions remind me of a familiar scripture:

"Then I heard a loud voice saying in heaven, "Now salvation, and strength, and the kingdom of our God, and the power of His Christ have come, for the accuser of our brethren, who accused them before our God day and night, has been cast down. And they overcame him by the blood of the Lamb and by the word of their testimony, and they did not love their lives to the death. Therefore rejoice, O heavens, and you who dwell in them! Woe to the inhabitants of the earth and the sea! For the devil has come down to you, having great wrath, because he knows that he has a short time."

—Revelation 12:10-12

Despite the dangers and the threats on their lives, Iraqis braved the polls in record numbers that day with more than eight million people voting nationwide. That is how important freedom is to these people.

Likewise, we as believers should be willing to brave the onslaught of enemy attacks on us spiritually to forge forward with what God has called us to do. Whenever God calls you to do something for Him that will impact the Kingdom of God, you can be sure that the enemy will not be far behind.

A good friend told me one time, "Be happy when the enemy attacks, that means you're doing something right. If you were not a threat, he wouldn't mess with you." How true for us all. The responsibility we have is to dig in and persevere through the attack. If we are well grounded when attacks come, we will be unmoved.

"Therefore whoever hears these sayings of Mine, and does them, I will liken him to a wise man who built his house on the rock: and the rain descended, the floods came, and the winds blew and beat on that house; and it did not fall, for it was founded on the rock. "But

everyone who hears these sayings of Mine, and does not do them, will be like a foolish man who built his house on the sand: and the rain descended, the floods came, and the winds blew and beat on that house; and it fell. And great was its fall."

—Matthew 7:24-27

The verse I used to open this devotion seems kind of funny if you just glance at it. Ox, what does an ox have to do with anything? This verse was Solomon's way of saying, "Hey, if you want to see growth, if you want to see progress, you will have to deal with the mess that many times will come with it." There may be stress or discomfort for a time, but those things are part of growing.

The whole time there was a mess. The whole time the enemy was on the rampage. The whole time I was one step away from throwing in the towel. In the end, God showed Himself to be both Lord and King over all. Remember, if you never attempt great things for God, things that seem way over your head, you'll never fully see what God can do through you. In reality, you do not really doubt yourself, you doubt Him.

The enemy will always be there, but God will always be more powerful and able to defeat the schemes and tricks that he throws your way. Be strong and courageous man and woman of God, the battle belongs to Him!

From the Battlefield,
Pastor Ryan

Application:

The true mark of maturity in a believer is displaying the fruit of the Spirit in all situations, specifically, contentment within circumstances. Strong believers find and see the perfect Will of God regardless of personal comfort, preferences, or expectations they may have about the outcome in a situation. The longer you walk with Christ the more you come to see that adversity is a frequent companion of victory. When we see God work great things in and through us we should always be ready should trial come knocking. Jesus said: "In this world you will have tribulation, but be of good cheer for I have overcome the world." (John 16:33)

Prayer:

Lord, I long to grow in my knowledge of You and Your will for my life. Help me to mature and become more deeply rooted in Your Word and ways with each passing day. I know that trials are unavoidable Lord, but please strengthen me spiritually and emotionally to endure and persevere through them when they come. Help me also Lord to not become discouraged when difficulty comes my way. My desire is to worship and praise Your Holy name in the good times and the bad times. This I do because You are worthy, not because I feel like it. I thank you for hearing my prayer.

In Jesus' Name, Amen.

Day 30

Death of a Regime!

"Most assuredly, I say to you, unless a grain of wheat falls into the ground and dies, it remains alone; but if it dies, it produces much grain."

—John 12:24

"Why stand we here idle? Is life so dear or peace so sweet as to be purchased at the price of chains and slavery? Forbid it, Almighty God. I know not what course others may take, but as for me, give me liberty or give me death!"

—Patrick Henry
Speech in Virginia Convention
March, 1775

28 February 2005

One thing for sure can be said of the foundation of our Nation; it came about by the shedding of blood and the pure determination of a people no longer willing to endure tyranny and oppression. Though many died to make this nation free, I venture to say I would have to look far and wide to find an American who lives in freedom who would not admit that the end result was worth the high cost.

Lee Greenwood, in his song, "God bless the USA" says, "And I'd gladly stand up, next to you and defend her still today. Cause there ain't no doubt I love this land, God bless the USA." I think this song rings very true for the majority of Americans. No price is too high to pay for our families and children to live freely and peacefully.

Sometimes in order for a better good to come forth, something must die. Not only is this true for nations and countries, it is also true of us personally and spiritually.

Nations are born on the backs of those who are willing to shed their blood; Christians are born on the back of the One who was willing to shed His own blood. In fact, the scriptures declare to us that without death there could be no forgiveness of sin:

> *"In fact, we can say that according to the law of Moses, nearly everything was purified by sprinkling with blood. Without the shedding of blood, there is no forgiveness of sins."*
> —Hebrews 9:22, NLT

Sometimes we don't always understand why things must happen the way they do. We wonder why ministries divide and people go in different directions. We wonder why loved ones sometimes die, seemingly before their time. We don't understand why we must give up so much to go with God down the road He has chosen for us. Sometimes we find that unless we are willing to die, we cannot truly live. Paul says in Galatians 2:20:

> *"I have been crucified with Christ; it is no longer I who live, but Christ lives in me; and the life which I now live in the flesh I live by faith in the Son of God, who loved me and gave Himself for me."*

And again in Philippians 1:21:

> *"For to me, to live is Christ, and to die is gain."*

Unless we are willing to die to ourselves, Christ really can't use us for His Kingdom. A self-centered, self-absorbed servant is in direct contradiction with itself, for it is impossible for us to focus upon the glorious face of Christ while still continuously looking at ourselves.

Christ will not compete for first place in your life, for there is nothing that is remotely in the same class as He. It is a competition of one—Christ and Christ alone. Jesus said that we are to take up our cross and follow Him:

"He who loves father or mother more than Me is not worthy of Me. And he who loves son or daughter more than Me is not worthy of Me. And he who does not take his cross and follow after Me is not worthy of Me. He who finds his life will lose it, and he who loses his life for My sake will find it."
—Matthew 10:37-39

It took the death of Moses and the other first generation Israelites for Joshua and the next generation to enter in and possess the Promised Land. It took the death of Saul for David to become the king. It took the death of King Uzziah for Isaiah to finally see the Lord "seated on the throne, high and lifted up..." John the Baptist declared,

"He must increase but I must decrease."
—John 3:30

Sometimes it takes the death of that which *was* in order for the Lord to bring forth that which *will be*. In order for the fruit of the harvest to come forth in our life the death of the seed must first occur. That which we have held on to must give way to the new thing that God has purposed for us.

We find this to be true in nearly every aspect of Christian life. When we come to know Him we find that old things must pass away and new things come forth. This is true of relationships, habits, hobbies, interests—practically everything. Jesus leaves no stone unturned in our lives because He desires to do more and more through us.

> *"Therefore, if anyone is in Christ, he is a new creation; old things have passed away; behold, all things have become new."*
> —2 Corinthians 5:17

We find this to even be true concerning the practice and symbolism of baptism. The symbolic death of the old nature is transformed into the emergence of the newly reborn child of God possessing and taking on the name and likeness of the Master.

> *"What shall we say then? Shall we continue in sin that grace may abound? Certainly not! How shall we who died to sin live any longer in it? Or do you not know that as many of us as were baptized into Christ Jesus were baptized into His death? Therefore we were buried with Him through baptism into death, that just as Christ was raised from the dead by the glory of the Father, even so we also should walk in newness of life."*
> —Romans 6:1-4

For Christians, death does not mean the end, rather the beginning of something new—the next chapter. Are you now faced with the death of something or someone you love? Know this, in Christ we have eternal hope and the assurance of greater things to come. You may have pain and sorrow through the night, but His mercy and joy comes in fresh each morning.

From the Battlefield,
Pastor Ryan

Application:

A big disadvantage that the enemies and persecutors of Christians have is that if they kill us, we win! We actually gain so much more by laying our lives down than we do by remaining on this earth. Paul exemplified this in his words to the Philippian church when he said, "For me to live is Christ and to die is gain." Now granted, no one wants to actually take the death step, but we should all be pursuing a "death" life! This means dying to self daily that Christ may dwell richly in us unhindered by our selfishness and self-centered will.

Prayer:

Lord, today I pray for a "dead man walking" type of mentality. That each day I would walk the pathway to self-denial giving You free reign in every area of my life. Help me to live out the words of Your servant John the Baptist who said, "He must increase, but I must decrease. Fill me with Your glorious Holy Spirit and enable me to be void of my own will. I want more and more of You visible through my life to those around me. As I decrease, increase my love for You and for the lost in this world. Mold me and make me more like Jesus I pray.

Amen.